GUIDELINES

PURIM

GUIDELINES

Over Two Hundred and Fifty
of the Most Commonly
Asked Questions about
PURIM

Rabbi Elozor Barclay
Rabbi Yitzchok Jaeger

TARGUM/FELDHEIM

First published 2001
Copyright © 2001 by E. Barclay & Y. Jaeger
ISBN 1-56871-259-6

All rights reserved

No part of this publication may be translated, reproduced, stored in a retrieval system, or transmitted in any form or by any means, electronic, mechanical, photocopying, recording, or otherwise, without prior permission in writing from the copyright holders.

Please address any questions or comments
regarding these books to the authors:
E. Barclay (02) 583 0914
Y. Jaeger (02) 583 4889
email: jaeger@barak-online.net

By the same authors:
GUIDELINES TO PESACH
GUIDELINES TO THE YOMIM NORAIM
GUIDELINES TO CHANUKAH

Please contact the authors for details regarding dedication opportunities for future volumes.

Published by:
Targum Press, Inc.
22700 W. Eleven Mile Rd.
Southfield, MI 48034
E-mail: targum@netvision.net.il
Fax toll free: (888) 298-9992

Distributed by:
Feldheim Publishers
200 Airport Executive Park
Nanuet, NY 10954
www.feldheim.com

Printed in Israel

הרב רפאל צבי ובר
רב דקהילת קמניץ
ונוה יעקב מזרח, ירושלים

י"ז כסלו תשס"ב
בס"ד

מכתב ברכה

שמחתי לראות קונטרס הלכות בשפה האנגלית שיצא לאור ע"י ידידי הרב ר' אלעזר ברקלי שליט"א והרב ר' יצחק ייגר שליט"א, והנני מכירם ויודעם בהשתדלות לאסוקי שמעתתא אליבא דהלכתא.

והנני מברכם שיקבלו דבריהם בביהמ"ד.

בברכת התורה,

צבי ובר

Rabbi Nachman Bulman
Yeshivat Ohr Somayach
Beit Knesset Nachliel

רב נחמן בולמן
מנהל רוחני ישיבת אור שמח
רב ק"ק נחליאל נוה יעקב מזרח

בע"ה

יום א', י"ז כסלו, תשס"ב פה עיה"ק ת"ו

Sunday, seventeenth of Kislev, 5762, the holy city of Yerushalayim.

I was delighted to see the fourth volume of the **Guidelines** series. The questions and answers in **Guidelines** provide a clear and easily understood format and clarify relevant halachic issues.

It is clear from the quality of this work that Rabbi Elozor Barclay and Rabbi Yitzchok Jaeger have invested great amounts of time and effort in their thorough investigation of these dinim. Every answer has been written carefully and thoughtfully, considering both the classic and the most up-to-date halachic authorities. The accurate Hebrew references will certainly be an invaluable aid for any reader who wishes to investigate further.

I highly recommend this book to any person who is truly searching to know the correct conduct.

Signed with admiration,

נחמן בולמן

מנהל רוחני ישיבת אור שמח
רב ק"ק נחליאל נוה יעקב מזרח ביום הנ"ל
ועיני נשואות לשמים להסכמת שוכן במרומים

RABBI ZEV LEFF
Rabbi of Moshav Matisyahu
Rosh Hayeshiva Yeshiva Gedola Matisyahu

בס"ד
ז' כסלו תשס"ב

Faithfulness and consistency are attributes of Hashem that we are commanded to emulate. Rabbi Elozor Barclay שליט"א and Rabbi Yitzchok Jaeger שליט"א have been faithfully consistent in producing the latest addition to their series of **Guidelines** - Guidelines to Purim.

This collection of the laws of Purim into a concise, well-structured and clear compendium will be a guide to those not proficient enough to study the original sources and an aid for review and clarity to those who do study the original sources.

May Hashem be faithful and consistent with the authors and give them the ability to continue to merit the community in magnifying and glorifying the Torah.

With Torah blessings,

Rabbi Zev Leff

Table of Contents

	Page
Foreword	11
Chapter One: The *Parshiyos*	13
Chapter Two: Fast of Esther	17
Chapter Three: The Half Shekel	23
Chapter Four: The Two Days of Purim	27
Chapter Five: The Laws of Purim	30
Chapter Six: Before the Megillah	36
Chapter Seven: Reading the Megillah	38
Chapter Eight: The *Brachos* of the Megillah	43
Chapter Nine: Hearing the Megillah	47
Chapter Ten: Gifts to the Poor	57
Chapter Eleven: Sending Food	63
Chapter Twelve: Feasting and Rejoicing	70
Chapter Thirteen: Travelling on Purim	79
Chapter Fourteen: Purim *Meshulash*	83
Glossary	90
Index	93
Hebrew Sources	100

Foreword

With praise and gratitude to Hashem we present a basic guide to the laws of Purim. Our books on the laws of Pesach, the Yomim Noraim and Chanukah were warmly received by the public, encouraging and motivating us to develop this fourth volume.

Rarely will a written work be a perfect substitute for a one-to-one discussion with a rav. The answer to a query often depends upon various factors that only further questioning can clarify. Even though much thought and effort has been invested in the phrasing and wording used, it is possible that *halachos* may be incorrectly applied or misunderstood. Accordingly, any doubts that arise should be discussed with one's local rav.

Our primary intent is to guide the reader through the maze of laws and customs that abound during these joyous days, hence the title GUIDELINES. The laws of Purim are numerous and complex and a person who is not familiar with them will certainly not be able to fulfill his obligation properly.

We would like to express our thanks to the *halachic* authorities who assisted in the preparation of this work. First and foremost we would like to express our appreciation to *HaGaon* Rav Nachman Bulman, *shlita*, whose decades of experience as a *posek* and community leader imbue this *sefer* with his invaluable perspective, reliability and practicality.

Two exceptional *Talmidei Chachomim* graciously took time from their busy schedules to help turn this book into a reality. Rav Yirmiyahu Kaganoff, *shlita*, thoroughly checked the entire manuscript, providing many invaluable comments and observations. Rav Yitzchok Kaufman, *shlita*, read through the entire text and made numerous valuable corrections and suggestions.

Thanks are also due to Rabbi Moshe Dombey and all the staff at Targum Press who have once again demonstrated their professional expertise with the production of this book.

It is our hope that in the merit of keeping the laws of Purim punctiliously, Hashem will perform miracles and wonders for us as He did for our ancestors in the days of old.

Elozor Barclay　　　　　　　　　　　　　　Yitzchok Jaeger

Yerushalayim, Teves 5762

Chapter One
The Four *Parshiyos*

1. What are the four *parshiyos* and their significance?

The Sages instituted the public reading of four special portions of the Torah before and during the month of Adar. They are:

- *Parshas Shekalim*. This recalls the mitzvah of the ancient half-shekel coin that was donated annually to the temple treasury for the purchase of the daily offerings (see also chapter three).

- *Parshas Zachor*. This is read to recall the incident when the evil nation of Amalek attacked the Jewish people shortly after the Exodus from Egypt. With this reading, we fulfill the Torah obligation of remembering to eradicate this evil nation.

- *Parshas Parah*. This discusses the preparation of the ashes of the *Parah Adumah* (red cow) that was used by the Jewish people to purify themselves before Pesach. By reading this *parsha*, we pray to Hashem that He purify us speedily with the final redemption.

- *Parshas HaChodesh*. This recalls the sanctification of the month of Nissan as the first of the months of the year.

2. May a child be called up to the Torah for these portions?

Although a boy below bar mitzvah may be called up for a regular *maftir*, he should not be called up for *Parshas Zachor* or *Parshas Parah*. It is preferable not to call up a boy below bar mitzvah for *Parshas Shekalim* or *Parshas HaChodesh*, but under extenuating circumstances one may be lenient. This is important to remember when planning a bar mitzvah. Some communities have the custom to call up the rav or another important person for all four portions.

3. Are women obligated to hear the four *parshiyos*?

Women are not obligated to hear *Parshas Shekalim*, *Parah* and *HaChodesh*. There is a dispute as to whether women are obligated to hear *Parshas Zachor*. Many women have the custom to make an effort to go to shul to hear *Parshas Zachor*.

4. What should one think when hearing *Parshas Zachor*?

One should have in mind to fulfill the Torah mitzvah of remembering the attack of Amalek and to obliterate that nation. When listening to the *brachos* that are recited before and after the reading, one should have in mind that they are being recited on behalf of the entire congregation.

5. Is it necessary to understand all the words of *Parshas Zachor*?

It is important to understand the general meaning of the portion. Therefore a person who does not understand Hebrew should read a translation before the reading in shul. It is praiseworthy to understand the meaning of every word.

6. Is it necessary to hear every word?

Yes, one must hear every word (see also question 130).

7. May a person listen to a reading if it is recited in a pronunciation different than his own (*Ashkenazic, Sephardic, Chassidic* etc)?

Ideally, a person should fulfill the mitzvah by listening to a reading in a pronunciation the same as his own. In extenuating circumstances, he may listen to a reading in a different pronunciation.

8. What if a person missed *Parshas Zachor*?

Such a person should either:
- Have in mind to fulfill the Torah obligation when hearing the Torah reading on Purim morning.
- Say the verses of *Parshas Zachor* from a *chumash*. If possible, he should sing the words with the tune of the Torah reading.

9. What should one think when hearing the other *parshiyos*?

Ideally, one should have in mind to fulfill the Rabbinic mitzvah to hear these *parshiyos*.

10. What if a man missed one of the other three *parshiyos*?

Nothing needs to be done.

Chapter Two

Fast of Esther

11. What is the meaning of this fast?

In the days of Mordechai and Esther (3405 from creation), the Jewish people assembled on the 13th of Adar to fight their enemies and defend their lives (see chapter four). In order to arouse the mercy and help of Hashem, they fasted and prayed, following in the footsteps of Moshe Rabbeinu who decreed a day of fasting when waging war with Amalek. The Fast of Esther reminds us that when a person fasts and repents sincerely, Hashem sees and delivers him from all troubles.

12. Is this a suitable day for private prayers?

This day is extremely appropriate for private prayers and the gates of Heaven are open. One should first say Psalm 22, which by tradition was composed by Esther, and then pour out one's heart with personal requests. One should conclude with a request to be answered in the merit of Mordechai and Esther.

13. Do women need to fast?

Girls over bas mitzvah and women are obligated to fast if they are well. If they are weak or find fasting difficult, they need not fast. Certain communities are lenient in this matter, and are strict only on Yom Kippur and Tisha b'Av.

14. Do pregnant or nursing women need to fast?

No. The laws of this fast are more lenient than for other fasts, and women who are pregnant or nursing are exempt even if they feel well.

15. What if a person is not feeling well?

A person who is ill is not permitted to fast even if his illness is not serious. Even if one has only a severe headache he should not fast, and if he has been fasting he should break the fast.

16. Should children be trained to fast?

No, children below bar or bas mitzvah do not need to fast even for a few hours. Nevertheless, they should not be given treats.

17. If a person is not required to fast, should he delay eating for a few hours?

No, this is not necessary and he may eat immediately in the morning.

18. May such a person eat as much as he likes?

No. In order to participate in the public fast day, he should limit himself to a sufficient amount of simple foods.

19. Is there anything that can be done in place of fasting by someone who is exempt?

- A person who is unwell and therefore exempt from fasting may fast on another day in place of this communal fast. Alternatively, money can be given to charity.
- Pregnant and nursing women need not do anything.

20. How should a person who is fasting take medicine if required?

A person may swallow bitter or tasteless medicines in tablet, capsule or liquid form, but not if they are pleasant tasting. The medicine should be taken without water. If one cannot swallow the capsule without any liquid, he should use a bitter tasting liquid e.g. lemon juice. (If the capsule will still be effective when the contents are mixed with water, this is a practical solution since such liquid is usually bitter tasting.)

21. Is a person who is fasting permitted to taste food and spit it out?

This is usually forbidden. However, it is permitted to taste a small quantity of food that is being prepared for a *seudas mitzvah* after the fast. One should spit out the food and be careful not to swallow any.

22. May the mouth be rinsed?

One may rinse the mouth only if a bad taste causes discomfort. Only a small amount of liquid should be used while leaning forwards in order to minimize the chance of it being swallowed.

23. May the teeth be cleaned?
The teeth may be cleaned with a dry toothbrush.

24. May one eat early in the morning before the fast begins?
The fast begins at *halachic* dawn and it is permitted to eat until this time. However, before going to sleep the previous evening one must have in mind that he wishes to eat before dawn. A person who happens to wake up early unexpectedly and did not intend to eat before dawn may not do so. However if a person forgot or woke up unexpectedly, he may **drink** before dawn, even though it is still preferable to have it in mind from the previous evening.

25. How close to *halachic* dawn may one eat?
If one wishes to eat bread or cake, he must begin at least thirty minutes before *halachic* dawn. One may begin to eat other foods or drinks even within this period. Women are not restricted by this thirty-minute limit even for bread or cake.

26. If a person made a *b'racha* on food or drink and then realized that it is a fast day, what should he do?
He must say ברוך שם כבוד מלכותו לעולם ועד and not eat or drink anything.

27. If a person accidentally ate or drank what should he do?

He must stop immediately and continue to fast for the rest of the day. He is not obligated to fast on another day. If he wishes to gain atonement for his mistake he may fast on another day but if this is difficult he may give a reasonable sum of money to charity.

28. May such a person still say *aneinu* in the *Shemoneh Esrei*?

Yes, but he should alter the wording slightly and say 'ביום צוֹם התענית הזה'.

29. May a person who is exempt from fasting (e.g. ill, pregnant, a child etc.) say *aneinu* in the *Shemoneh Esrei*?

No, the paragraph is omitted completely.

30. What should a person do if he forgot to say *aneinu*?

If he has already concluded the *b'racha* of שומע תפלה he should continue and say *aneinu* just before the verse יהיו לרצון at the end of *Shemoneh Esrei*. If he forgot there also, *Shemoneh Esrei* is not repeated.

31. Is there any other change to the *Shemoneh Esrei* on a fast day?

Yes. Instead of saying שלום רב at *mincha*, שים שלום should be said, even if one is not fasting and even if one is not *davening* with a *minyan*. In addition, a person who is fasting should say a special prayer before the end of *Shemoneh Esrei*. This begins רבון כל העולמים גלוי וידוע לפניך.

32. Is אבינו מלכנו recited at *mincha*?

When the fast is on the 13th of Adar, אבינו מלכנו is not said at *mincha*, since it is *erev* Purim. When the 13th of Adar is on Shabbos and the fast is brought forward to the preceding Thursday, אבינו מלכנו is recited.

33. Can the prayer אבינו מלכנו be said without a *minyan* or if one is not fasting?

Yes.

34. Is bathing permitted?

Bathing is permitted even with hot water. Although this is forbidden on *Tisha B'Av* and customarily not done on the other Rabbinic fasts, it is permitted on the Fast of Esther since it is not a day of mourning.

35. May one listen to music?

Yes, this is permitted since it is not a day of mourning.

36. Is there any special mitzvah performed on this day?

Yes. The mitzvah known as *machatzis haShekel* is performed on the Fast of Esther (see chapter three). In Jerusalem, some have the custom to perform it on the 14th of Adar.

Chapter Three
The Half Shekel

37. What is the meaning of the *machatzis haShekel*?

On *erev* Purim, there is a custom to give three coins to charity, to recall the half-shekel that was donated annually to the Temple treasury in the month of Adar. Each coin should be the denomination of half the standard currency in that country (e.g. half a shekel, half a dollar, half a pound).

38. Why are three coins given?

In the portion of the Torah dealing with the half-shekel (*Shemos* 30, 11-16) the word '*terumah*' - donation appears three times.

39. Must one give precisely these three half coins?

Yes. One should not give one whole coin and one half coin, nor give more than the correct amount and take change. If a person does not have the correct coins he should obtain them from another person or from the charity box.

40. What if one cannot obtain the exact coins anywhere?

He should give three whole coins and have in mind that half of each coin is to fulfill the mitzvah, and the other halves are a gift to charity. Alternatively, two people could join together to give three whole coins.

41. Must the half coins have a minimum value?

Strictly speaking, there is no minimum requirement and one may even use half coins of low value. However, in this situation it is praiseworthy to give a sum of money equal to the value of the original half shekel, in addition to the three coins. This is approximately two dollars (9.6 grams of silver). If a person gives several sets of half coins for family members (see question 44) and the total value reaches this figure, he is not required to give more.

42. What if there is no half coin in the local currency?

He should use the suggestions mentioned above in question 40.

43. May one use coins of another country?

It is questionable whether a person may use coins that are not legal tender in his own country. He should use one of the suggestions mentioned above and under extenuating circumstances one can fulfill this mitzvah by giving any sum of money to charity.

44. Who is obligated to fulfill this mitzvah?

According to one opinion, only men from age twenty are obligated, and according to another opinion, all men above bar mitzvah are obligated. However, the custom is that a father gives on behalf of all his sons, whatever their ages. The custom is also to give for one's wife who is pregnant, in case the child is a boy.

45. Are women obligated to give?

According to the accepted custom, women do not give.

46. May a person change his custom?

If a person began to give on behalf of his wife or children, he must continue to do so always. Even annulment of vows may not be performed. This does not obligate him to give on behalf of those for whom he never gave. If he began to give on behalf of his wife or children with the mistaken assumption that this is an obligation, he may discontinue the practice without annulment of vows.

47. Should the money be given to a specific cause?

The money should be given to the poor. It should not be used for shul upkeep, communal needs or a similar cause.

48. What if one cannot find a poor person?

The money should be set aside for the poor and kept until he is able to give it to the correct cause.

49. On which day is the mitzvah performed?

On the fast of Esther. In Jerusalem, some have the custom to perform it on the 14th of Adar.

50. When during the day should the mitzvah be performed?

At *mincha* time. Some perform the mitzvah before *mincha* and some perform it afterwards.

51. What if one forgot to perform the mitzvah on the correct day?

He should give the money on Purim morning, before the megillah is read. If he forgot then also, he may give it until the end of Adar.

52. Should anything be said when giving the money?

Nothing needs to be said, but if one wishes one may say that this is to commemorate the giving of the half-shekel. One must be careful not to say, "this **is** the half-shekel", since according to some opinions, this would sanctify the money and prohibit its use.

53. May one use *ma'aser* money?

No. *Ma'aser* money may not be used to fulfill an obligation or an accepted custom but rather is reserved for voluntary donations to charity. (See also questions 172, 197).

Chapter Four
The Two Days of Purim

54. Why are there two days of Purim?

In most of the world, Purim is celebrated on the 14th of Adar, but in Jerusalem and a few other places it is celebrated on the 15th. This difference is because of the way in which the miracle occurred. The wicked Haman, a descendant of Amalek, had enacted a decree signed by the King Achashverosh, to kill all the Jews on the 13th of Adar. When this day arrived, the Jewish people defended their lives and waged war against their enemies throughout the 127 provinces of the kingdom. A great miracle occurred and the tables were completely turned. Thousands of Amalekites were killed and not a single Jew lost his life. The following day, the 14th of Adar, was celebrated everywhere as a day of great rejoicing. However, in Shushan the capital, the fighting continued on the 14th of Adar at the request of Esther, and the 15th of Adar became a day of rejoicing. The Sages wished to commemorate these events by fixing two different days for Purim.

55. What is the criterion for fixing the day of Purim?

Since Shushan was a walled city, the Sages decided to give special status to any city that was walled during the days of Joshua. Such a city celebrates Purim on the

15th of Adar, as does Shushan itself. One may have expected the criterion to be dependent on the city having a wall during the days of Esther, but *Eretz Yisrael* was desolate at that time and walled cities in *chutz la'aretz* would have received the honor. Therefore the time of Joshua was chosen as the criterion in order to bestow special honor to *Eretz Yisrael*. Shushan, where the miracle occurred became an exception to the rule, celebrating Purim on the 15th of Adar, even though it was not walled during the days of Joshua. It is for this reason that the 15th of Adar is known as Shushan Purim.

56. Which cities celebrate the 15th of Adar today?

- Today, only Jerusalem celebrates Purim on the 15th of Adar.
- A number of cities in *Eretz Yisrael* observe both days because of doubts about the existence of walls during that period. These places include Acco, Beer-Sheva, Haifa, Jaffa, Lod, and Safed. Hebron and Tiberias have the custom to observe both days only for the mitzvah of the megillah. In *chutz la'aretz*, Baghdad, Damascus and Prague read the megillah on both days. In all these places, the *brachos* for the megillah are recited on the 14th of Adar only.

57. Should all neighborhoods in Jerusalem observe Purim on the 15th of Adar?

Even though most Jerusalem neighborhoods lie outside the walls of the old city, almost all neighborhoods

Chapter Four – The Two Days of Purim 29

observe the 15th. This is because the city extends beyond the walls in all directions with residential areas adjacent to one another, thereby uniting all neighborhoods into one big city. Outlying isolated areas that are separated from the city by a distance of 141 cubits (approx. 80 meters) may be considered a separate town that should observe the 14th. A rav must be consulted in this situation.

58. Do places that observe the 14th celebrate in any way on the 15th and vice-versa?

The following apply to everyone in all places on both days:
- Rejoicing and festive eating (see next question).
- Prohibition to fast and eulogize.
- Omitting *Tachanun* and *lamnatzeach*.

59. Should one feast and rejoice equally on both days?

No. The main feasting and rejoicing is reserved for the main day of Purim that one observes. A person should feast and rejoice a little more than usual on the other day of Purim.

Chapter Five

The Laws of Purim

60. What mitzvos are performed on Purim?

There are four mitzvos to perform:
- Reading the megillah night and day (see chapter seven).
- Giving gifts to the poor (see chapter ten).
- Sending food packages to one another (see chapter eleven).
- Feasting and rejoicing (see chapter twelve).

61. What are the main changes to the prayers on Purim?

- *Tachanun* and *lamnatzeach* are omitted.
- The Torah is read.
- *Al haNissim* is added to the *Shemoneh Esrei* and *bensching*.

62. Where is *al haNissim* recited in *Shemoneh Esrei*?

It is said during the *b'racha* of *Modim*. In it, we thank Hashem for the miracles that he performed and for rescinding the decree of the evil Haman.

63. Should one say על הניסים or ועל הניסים?

Both versions are acceptable. According to some opinions, 'ועל' is more correct.

64. May one say *al haNissim* by heart?

Since this has not been said for an entire year, one should use a *siddur* at least the first time, in order to prevent mistakes.

65. What if one forgot to say it?

- If he has not yet said the name of Hashem at the conclusion of the *b'racha*, he should go back to *al haNissim* and continue from there.
- If he has already said Hashem's name he should continue the *Shemoneh Esrei*. At the end of the paragraph א-להי נצור before saying the verse יהיו לרצון he should add a special prayer;

"יהי רצון מלפניך שתעשה לנו נסים ונפלאות כשם שעשית לאבותינו בימים ההם בזמן הזה".

He should then continue בימי מרדכי.

66. What if he forgot to say this special prayer?

He does not repeat *Shemoneh Esrei*.

67. Where is *al haNissim* added to *bensching*?

In the second *b'racha*.

68. What if one forgot to say it?

- If he has not yet said the name of Hashem at the conclusion of the *b'racha*, he should go back to *al haNissim* and continue again from there.
- If he has already said the name of Hashem he should continue *bensching*. Upon reaching the special

haRachaman prayers that are recited on Shabbos and *Yom Tov*, he should add a special prayer:

"הרחמן הוא יעשה לנו נסים ונפלאות כשם שעשה לאבותינו בימים ההם בזמן הזה".

He should then continue בימי מרדכי.

69. If one forgets *al haNissim* on Shabbos, where should the special *haRachaman* be inserted (this can only occur in Jerusalem)?

After the *haRachaman* for Shabbos.

70. What if he forgot the special *haRachaman*?

He does not repeat *bensching*. This is the case even on *Shabbos*.

71. Why is *hallel* not said?

Three reasons are given for this:
- The megillah reading is in place of *hallel*.
- *Hallel* is only said to celebrate a miracle that resulted in our freedom to serve Hashem, but after the miracle of Purim we still remained enslaved to Achashverosh.
- *Hallel* can only be said for a miracle that occurred in *Eretz Yisrael*, but the miracle of Purim occurred in Persia.

72. May a person *daven* while dressed in fancy costume?

This is forbidden since one must dress respectably when *davening*. In addition, the custom is to wear Shabbos clothes on Purim (see question 84).

73. May a person *daven* while intoxicated?

- If he is intoxicated to the extent that he would not be able to speak respectfully to an important official, he may not *daven*. A prayer recited in such a state is an abomination, and there is an obligation to *daven* again when sober.
- If he is only slightly intoxicated, to the extent that he would be able to speak respectfully to an important official, it is nonetheless not correct to *daven*. However, the custom on Purim is to be lenient and allow prayer in this state, although ideally he should wait until he is sober.
- A person who is careful not to *daven* while intoxicated will be saved from all troubles.

74. What if the final time to *daven* will pass before he is sober?

If he is very intoxicated he may not *daven*, but when he becomes sober he should make up the missed prayer by saying *Shemoneh Esrei* twice at the next service. If he is only slightly intoxicated he may *daven* if the time of prayer will pass.

75. May a person do work on Purim?

The custom is to prohibit work on Purim. Whoever works on Purim will not see any blessing from it.

76. Are there any cases when it is permitted to work?

Work is permitted in the following situations:
- If not working will cause financial loss.
- Making business deals that will give pleasure.
- Work that is necessary for a mitzvah.
- Work that is required for Purim.
- Simple jobs that do not require much concentration. Care should be taken not to become too involved with the job and be distracted from the merriment of the day.

77. May one ask a gentile to do work for him?

Yes, all forms of work are permitted through a gentile.

78. Is it permitted to launder?

Laundering is forbidden unless the clothes are needed on Purim.

79. May one shave or have a haircut?

It is permitted when done in order to look presentable for Purim itself, but not because one has spare time on Purim.

Chapter Five – The Laws of Purim

80. May one cut his nails?

Cutting nails is forbidden. When Purim is on Friday, it is permitted in honor of Shabbos.

81. Is writing permitted?

Only the following writing is permitted:
- Simple Torah notes.
- Letters to friends.
- A reminder of one's debts.
- Any short notes.

82. Do these restrictions apply on the evening of Purim?

According to the generally accepted opinion, all forms of work are permitted in the evening.

83. Do these restrictions also apply on the 15th of Adar (and on the 14th in Jerusalem)?

The accepted custom is to permit all work on the other day of Purim.

84. Should one wear Shabbos clothes on Purim?

The custom is to wear Shabbos clothes on Purim. One should change into Shabbos clothes on the evening of Purim before hearing the megillah.

Chapter Six
Before the Megillah

85. May one eat before hearing the megillah?

Under normal circumstances, it is forbidden to eat or drink before the megillah, both at night and during the day.

86. From what time in the evening does this restriction begin?

From half-an-hour before nightfall. This is particularly important for people who are not fasting and for those who observe Purim on the 15th of Adar.

87. What if a person is sick or weak?

A person who is sick or weak because of the fast may eat cake or bread up to the size of an egg (57cc). Other foods and non-alcoholic drinks may be consumed without limitation.

88. What if a person needs to eat or drink more than this quantity of bread or cake?

He may eat if he asks another person who is not eating to remind him to hear the megillah.

Chapter Six – Before the Megillah

89. Does this restriction apply to women also?

Yes. However, since a woman often hears the megillah later in the evening and morning, she may eat earlier if she asks her husband to remind her to hear the megillah.

90. May one sleep before hearing the megillah?

Within half-an-hour before nightfall, even a short nap is forbidden. It is permitted if another person is asked to remind him to hear the megillah and to wake him up if necessary.

91. May one do work before hearing the megillah?

It is forbidden to start activities that
- take more than a few minutes **or**
- have a tendency to continue for some time **or**
- are hard to break off in the middle.

92. May one learn Torah before hearing the megillah?

Yes.

Chapter Seven

Reading the Megillah

93. Why is the megillah read twice - at night and again in the morning?

This is to recall the miracle that occurred through the Jews crying out in their troubles by day and by night.

94. What is the earliest time it may be read at night?

The correct time is after nightfall. In extenuating circumstances, it may be read earlier. If a person is suffering because of the fast it is better to eat a small quantity of food (see question 87) and read the megillah only after nightfall than to read the megillah early and eat afterwards.

95. What is the latest time it may be read at night?

It must be read before *halachic* dawn. It is praiseworthy to read the megillah immediately after *ma'ariv*, since one should endeavor to perform all mitzvos at the first possible opportunity.

96. What if a person missed the night reading?

The mitzvah cannot be made up by reading the megillah twice during the day (see also question 101).

97. What is the earliest time for the daytime reading?

The correct time is after sunrise. In an unavoidable situation, it may be read after *halachic* dawn.

98. What is the latest time for the daytime reading?

It must be read before sunset. If a person did not read or hear the megillah before sunset, he should nevertheless read it before nightfall, but without reciting the *brachos*. He should also omit the *brachos* if he begins to read before sunset but will not complete the reading until after sunset.

99. If a person knows in advance that he will not be able to hear the megillah on Purim (e.g. he is scheduled for surgery on that day, travelling etc.) what can be done?

He should read the megillah (from a kosher scroll) at night and during the day on the 11th, 12th, or 13th of Adar. The *brachos* should not be recited. If this too is impossible, he may even read it from *rosh chodesh* Adar. It should preferably be read in the presence of ten people.

100. What if subsequently it becomes possible to read the megillah on Purim?

He must hear the megillah again on Purim with *brachos*.

101. What if a person accidentally missed both megillah readings on the 14th of Adar?

- It is praiseworthy to be in Jerusalem on the 15th of Adar (see chapter thirteen).
- If this is not possible, he should read the megillah on the 15th without *brachos*. Preferably, it should be read in the presence of ten people.

102. Are women obligated to hear the megillah?

Yes. Although this is a time-bound mitzvah, women are obligated, since they were also included in the decree and the miraculous salvation.

103. May a woman read the megillah for herself from a kosher megillah?

Ideally, a woman should hear the megillah read by a man. In extenuating circumstances she may read it for herself (see also question 119).

104. May a woman read the megillah for a man?

No, a man must hear it read by another man.

105. May a woman read it for another woman?

Yes, but she should not read it for a group of women.

106. Are children obligated to hear the megillah?

Children who are mature enough to listen attentively to the megillah reading should do so. Preferably, such children should be brought to shul to hear the public reading. However, they must be properly supervised during the reading and should understand that they have not been brought to shul simply for the fun of banging at Haman. Young children who are likely to cause a disturbance and prevent others from hearing the megillah should not be brought to shul.

107. May a child read the megillah for an adult?

Ideally, an adult should hear the megillah read by an adult. In extenuating circumstances, he may hear it read by a child.

108. Must the reader and listener be celebrating the same day of Purim?

Ideally, the reader and listener must be keeping the same day. However, if someone who is keeping the 14th heard the megillah on the 14th from someone who will keep the 15th, he has fulfilled his obligation. If someone keeping the 15th heard it on the 15th from someone who kept the 14th, he has not fulfilled his obligation. (Compare questions 185, 216.)

109. What must a person think before reading or listening to the megillah?

Men should have in mind that they are fulfilling the mitzvah to **read** the megillah. Women should have in mind that they are fulfilling the mitzvah to **hear** the megillah. Additionally, the reader should have in mind to include all the listeners who wish to fulfill their obligation.

110. Must one think about this throughout the reading?

No, it is sufficient to think this before the reading begins.

111. What if a person did not think about this?

If it is clear that he had this at the back of his mind, he has fulfilled his obligation. Therefore, the reader in shul is assumed to include all listeners and a person who comes to shul to hear the megillah is assumed to want to fulfill his obligation. The same applies when people gather in a house for the reading of the megillah.

112. When would the lack of thought invalidate the reading?

If it not clear from his actions that he intends to fulfill his obligation. For example;
- if he was passing by a shul or house and happened to overhear the reading, or
- if he reads the megillah in order to practice.

Chapter Eight
The *Brachos* of the Megillah

113. Which *brachos* are recited before the megillah reading?

Three *brachos* are recited:
- אשר קדשנו במצותיו וצונו על מקרא מגילה.
- שעשה ניסים.
- שהחיינו.

Ashkenazic congregations repeat all three *brachos* in the morning. *Sephardim* do not repeat *shehecheyanu* at the daytime reading.

114. What should one think about when listening to the *brachos*?

One should have in mind that he is fulfilling his obligation. When hearing the *shehecheyanu b'racha* during the day, one should have in mind to include all the special mitzvos of Purim. Those who have the custom not to repeat the *shehecheyanu b'racha* during the day should have these mitzvos in mind when hearing the *b'racha* in the evening.

115. What should the reader think about when reciting the *brachos*?

He should have in mind that he is reciting them on behalf of the entire congregation.

116. Who should say the *brachos* if the reader has already fulfilled his obligation?

Preferably the listeners should say the *brachos*. This is especially important when reading for women. However, many have the custom that the reader always says the *brachos*, whether reading for men or women.

117. If the listeners wish to say the *brachos* should one man say the *brachos* aloud for everyone?

If there are ten or more men listening, one man should say the *brachos* aloud for everyone. If there are less then ten men, each person should say the *brachos* for himself.

118. If ten or more women are listening should one woman say the *brachos* aloud for everyone?

One woman can say the *brachos* for all the women. According to some opinions, one woman should not say the *brachos* for the others but each woman should say the *brachos* herself.

119. Do women recite the same *brachos* as men?

There are different customs regarding the first *b'racha* and there are three possible texts:
- על מקרא מגילה (same as men).
- לשמוע מגילה.
- לשמוע מקרא מגילה.

120. May a mourner read the megillah in shul?

A mourner may not say the *shehecheyanu b'racha* on behalf of the congregation, therefore it is preferable for someone else to read the megillah. If the regular reader became a mourner he may read the megillah as usual, but another person should say the *brachos*.

121. What if a person arrived in the middle of the *brachos*?

If there is sufficient time, he should quickly say the *brachos* himself, taking care that they are completed before the reading begins. If there is insufficient time to recite all of the *brachos*, he should say as many of the *brachos* as he can. If there is not enough time to recite any of the *brachos*, he should preferably attend another reading where he will hear the *brachos*. If this is very inconvenient, he may remain to listen to the megillah without *brachos*.

122. What if a person who is reading the megillah for himself forgot to recite the *brachos*?

If he remembers during the reading, he should say the *brachos* between the paragraphs (i.e. where there are spaces in the hand-written megillah).

123. Is a *b'racha* recited after the megillah reading?

An after *b'racha* is said only when the megillah is read in the presence of a *minyan*.

124. Is this *b'racha* recited when ten women hear the megillah?

There are different customs about this. The prevalent custom is to omit it.

125. Should anything be said in its place?

The *b'racha* should be said without the names of Hashem. It is correct to say the lines '*Shoshanas Ya'akov*'.

126. Must one stand when saying or hearing the *brachos*?

Yes, a person should stand if he is able.

Chapter Nine
Hearing the Megillah

127. If a person will be able to hear the megillah only once, is it better to hear the daytime reading or the night-time one?

It is preferable to hear it at night, since one should not postpone an opportunity to perform a mitzvah.

128. Must one stand during the reading of the megillah?

A person listening may sit. The reader should stand when reading to a *minyan*, but may lean if necessary. When reading to individuals, he may sit.

129. Must the reader stand when reading to ten women?

He should preferably stand.

130. Must one hear every word of the megillah?

Yes. If a person missed even one word he has not fulfilled his obligation (see also question 6).

131. What should a person do if he did not hear some words?

He should immediately say the words himself. However, this creates a problem since the reader continues to read the megillah while this person is saying the missed words, thereby causing him to miss further words. Therefore he must say the missed words and continue reading until he overtakes the reader, at which point he may resume listening.

132. May the missed words be said from a printed megillah?

If possible, a person should try to follow the reading in a kosher hand-written megillah, in order to be able to say the missed words from it. However, even if a person has a printed megillah, he may say the missed words from it and fulfill his obligation.

133. What if a person missed a word but did nothing about it?

- If he took his mind off the megillah, he must read or hear the megillah again from the beginning.
- If he did not take his mind off the megillah, he must read or hear the megillah from the missed word and onwards.

134. In these cases should the *brachos* be repeated?

The brachos should be repeated if he took his mind off the reading **and** the omission of the word caused a change or loss of meaning to the sentence.

135. What if a person did not hear a syllable (or the reader occasionally swallowed a syllable)?

If the word changes or loses its meaning it must be repeated, otherwise it need not be repeated.

136. What if a person is unsure whether he heard every word?

If he has a serious doubt whether he fulfilled his obligation, he must make an effort to read or hear the megillah again. The *brachos* should not be repeated.

137. Is it preferable to say the words quietly along with the reader?

- If a person is following with a printed megillah he must not say the words with the reader. This is because he may pay more attention to his own reading than to the words of the reader.
- If he is following with a hand-written megillah he may either listen or say the words along with the reader. Even if he chooses to read along, he should have in mind to fulfill his obligation through listening to the reader, except for any missed words which he fulfills through his own reading. Care should be taken not to disturb other people who wish to listen to the reader.

138. What if a person's mind wanders during the reading?

If his mind wanders completely to other things he does not fulfill his obligation, but if he is still partially concentrating on the megillah, he fulfills his obligation.

139. What is meant by partial concentration?

Partial concentration means that he would be able to answer the question 'What was read just now?'

140. How can one maintain concentration for the entire reading?

It is strongly recommended to keep one's finger on the page throughout the reading. Parents should not bring young children who need constant attention, since this will certainly interfere with their concentration.

141. May one listen to the megillah via telephone, loudspeaker or radio broadcast?

A person cannot fulfill his obligation by these methods. The sound that is heard from such machines is not a human voice but a recreated electronic voice. Such a sound is not valid for the mitzvah.

142. May one listen to the megillah with the assistance of a hearing aid?

In this case too the sound heard via the hearing aid is not valid and the hearing aid should be removed. If a person cannot hear at all without the hearing aid, he should read the megillah himself.

143. Must one understand every word of the megillah?

No, a person fulfills his obligation even if he does not understand the words. However, a person who does not know Hebrew should read a translation beforehand in order to understand the story. This will enhance his concentration and he will have a greater appreciation of the miraculous events.

144. What if a person needs to use the bathroom during the reading?

A person who needs to use the bathroom is permitted to remain until the end of the megillah. If he is reading for himself, he may stop to use the bathroom and continue from where he left off. The *b'racha* אשר יצר should be recited at the end of the reading.

145. May one speak during the megillah reading?

It is forbidden for both the reader and the listener to speak from the beginning of the first *b'racha* until the end of the after *b'racha*. Parents must be aware of this when bringing young children to the reading.

146. What if the reader spoke during the reading?

The reading is still valid.

147. What if a listener spoke during the reading?

If he did not miss any words (i.e. he spoke during a break in the reading) he fulfilled his obligation. If he missed a word, he did not fulfill his obligation unless he corrected the situation (see questions 131-134).

148. What if the listener paid attention to the reading while he was speaking?

He did not fulfill his obligation unless he corrected the situation (see questions 131-134). This is particularly important for parents who may need to speak to their children during the reading.

149. Must the megillah be said in its correct tune?

Ideally, it should be sung with the traditional tune. If a person must read the megillah but does not know the tune, he may say the words. An inexperienced reader must take care not to make any reading mistakes. It is advisable to ask someone else to listen and correct any errors.

150. Why are certain verses said aloud by the congregation?

There are several reasons:
- These are crucial points in the story, marking the beginning or end of a miracle.
- To arouse the interest of the children.
- To express joy.

151. Which verses are said aloud by the congregation?

- איש יהודי (chapter 2, verse 5).
- ומרדכי יצא (chapter 8, verse 15).
- ליהודים היתה (chapter 8, verse 16).
- כי מרדכי (chapter 10, verse 3).

152. Why are the names of the ten sons of Haman customarily said aloud by the congregation?

Two reasons are given for this:
- All ten names should be read in one breath to indicate that they were all slain and hung together, and this should be done by each individual.
- The reader is inclined to rush through the names and the listeners may not hear every word clearly.

153. What if a person did not succeed in saying all the names in one breath?

He need not repeat them.

154. Why does the reader repeat these verses and the ten names after the congregation?

This is for the benefit of those who are reading from a printed megillah.

155. Why does the reader read certain verses twice?

In two places in the megillah there are two versions of the text. In order to say both versions, the verses are read twice. In some communities, only that phrase is repeated.

156. Which verses are they?
- להרוג, ולהרוג (chapter 8, verse 11).
- בפניהם, לפניהם (chapter 9, verse 2).

157. Why is the megillah spread out wide and doubled over?
There are two reasons:
- The megillah is called a letter (chapter 9, verse 26) and when a person reads a letter he spreads it out completely.
- To make greater publicity of the miracle.

158. Should everyone spread open his megillah?
The prevalent custom is that only the reader does so, but not the listeners. When the megillah is read privately to individuals, the custom is that even the reader does not spread it open.

159. If the after *b'racha* is said, should the megillah be rolled up first?
Yes. The megillah should be rolled up before saying the after *b'racha*.

160. Should the banging at 'Haman' be discouraged?
One should not abolish or scorn any Jewish custom, since it is sure to have a valid basis. This custom is

based upon the mitzvah to eradicate the memory of Amalek (see questions 1 and 4). Originally, children would write the name 'Haman' or draw his picture on pieces of wood and stone. When the pieces were banged together the name or the picture would be obliterated. Nevertheless, excessive noise and tumult should be discouraged since this often prevents people from hearing clearly.

161. If the shul reading is extremely noisy may one stay at home and read it privately?

In order to enhance the mitzvah and make greater publicity of the miracle, both men and women should make every effort to attend the public reading in shul. Even if one can organize a minyan at home, it is better to join the congregation. If a person has difficulty hearing every word in shul, he should say those words himself (see question 131). If he knows that it is impossible to hear the reading in shul, he should attend a private reading.

162. What if a person cannot go to shul?

He may read or listen to the megillah being read privately. Nevertheless, it would be praiseworthy to gather ten men or women to attend the reading in order to enhance the mitzvah. It does not matter if these people have already heard the megillah.

163. May the reader use a printed megillah?

No, one may not fulfill the mitzvah by reading from a printed megillah. The mitzvah must be performed by reading a kosher megillah, hand-written on parchment.

164. What if a few letters are cracked or erased?

Ideally, one should use a megillah in which every letter is written clearly. If such a megillah is unobtainable, one may read from a hand-written megillah that has several erasures (see also next question). The *brachos* should be said as usual.

165. How many erasures are permitted?

As long as the majority is written clearly the reader may use such a megillah. However, if an entire section is missing, **or** if the first or last verse is missing, the megillah may not be used.

Chapter Ten
Gifts to the Poor

166. How does one perform this mitzvah?
On the day of Purim, one must give one gift each to at least two poor people.

167. What type of gift should be given?
The gift may be either money or food.

168. How much food or money must one give?
Each poor person should be given at least the amount of food that is usually eaten at a regular meal or the amount of money required to buy this.

169. Is it recommended to give more than this?
It is better to spend more on this mitzvah than on *mishloach manos* (sending food packages) and the Purim meal. There is no greater joy than gladdening the hearts of orphans, widows and needy people. One who does so is likened to Hashem, as it says about Him 'to revive the spirit of the humble and to revive the heart of the downtrodden' (Isiah 57, 15).

170. Is it better to give two large donations or many small ones?

Since the primary objective is to bring joy to the poor, it is preferable to give two large donations. This will bring more joy to the recipients than if one would give many insignificant donations.

171. May one give a check?

A check may be given if it can easily be exchanged for cash, through a bank or another person.

172. May one use *ma'aser* money?

Ma'aser money may be used for any donation except for the minimum two gifts (see also questions 53, 197).

173. Are women obligated to give?

Yes, since they were also included in the Purim miracle.

174. May a married woman rely on her husband to give on her behalf?

Although the custom is to rely on this, nevertheless it is preferable for her to perform the mitzvah personally.

175. How could a wife do this personally?

There are two options:
- The husband could give his wife some money explicitly for her own personal use. The wife can then give this money to two poor people through the husband or a charity collector.
- The husband could give some money to a charity collector stating that this is on behalf of his

wife. The charity collector should have in mind to acquire the money on behalf of the woman, and she should know that this procedure is being used for her.

176. How should children living at home perform the mitzvah?

They should use one of the above methods.

177. Are children below bar or bas mitzvah obligated in this mitzvah?

Children aged six or seven should be trained to perform this mitzvah. One of the above methods should be used.

178. What if one does not know who is qualified to receive the gifts?

One should give the money to an authorized charity collector who will distribute the money on Purim for the purpose of fulfilling this mitzvah.

179. Should one give two separate sums to the charity collector for two different people?

If the charity collector will divide the money between at least two poor people, one may give a single sum to him to be divided among the recipients. If the money will be given to one poor person only, one must give another amount to another collector.

180. When is the correct time to perform the mitzvah?

The mitzvah should be performed on Purim during the daytime. It is preferable to do it after the megillah reading without delay, so that the *shehecheyanu b'racha* can apply to it (see question 114).

181. Can one fulfill this mitzvah on the evening of Purim or earlier?

If a person gives the money (or food) to a poor person on the evening of Purim or earlier he does not fulfill his obligation. However, if he stipulates that the money (or food) must only be used on the day of Purim, he has fulfilled his obligation according to some opinions.

182. May one give the money to a charity collector before Purim?

This may be done if the charity collector will distribute the money to the poor people only on the day of Purim for the purpose of fulfilling this mitzvah. The collector should not acquire the money on behalf of the poor when he accepts it, but should act as a guardian of the money until it is delivered.

183. What if a charity collector is unable to deliver the money on Purim?

Every effort should be made to deliver it on Purim so that the poor people can have the joy of receiving the money on Purim. If this is not possible, the collector should acquire the money on behalf of the poor on Purim, and this is considered as if the poor have already received it. The mitzvah would be enhanced if the collector would at least notify the poor about the money, in order to give them some degree of joy on Purim.

184. What if a person cannot find a poor person or a charity collector?

If a person anticipates this happening, he should send money before Purim to a poor person or a charity collector. Alternatively, he may call a friend on Purim asking him to donate money on his behalf, and reimburse the friend after Purim. If both methods are impossible, he should set aside the money on Purim and deliver it to the poor after Purim.

185. May a person observing the 14th give to a poor person who is observing the 15th, or vice-versa?

According to some opinions, the donor and recipient must observe the same day of Purim. According to other opinions, as long as the poor person receives the money on his day of Purim the donor has fulfilled his obligation. (Compare questions 108, 216.)

186. Must one give money to anyone who asks for charity?

During the entire year a person is not obligated to give charity to all who ask. He is entitled to investigate the worthiness of each cause and decide which charities deserve priority. On Purim however, one may not refuse any person who may be in a state of poverty and at least a small donation should be given unquestioningly. Whoever gives charity on Purim with an open hand brings great light to the higher worlds and annuls evil decrees.

187. Must one also give to gentiles?
Only if the local custom is to do so.

188. Must one also give to children under bar mitzvah?
No, unless one seriously suspects that they are poor.

Chapter Eleven

Sending Food

189. How does one perform this mitzvah?

On the day of Purim, one must send two items of food to at least one person.

190. What is the reason for this mitzvah?

Two reasons are given:
- To ensure that everyone has sufficient food for the Purim feast.
- To increase love and friendship between Jews, thereby counterbalancing Haman's accusations that there is strife and dissention among Jews.

191. Is it praiseworthy to send to many people?

Yes, it is praiseworthy, but see also question 169.

192. Are all types of food suitable?

Preferably, one should send food that is ready to be eaten immediately. For example, raw meat, fish etc. which requires cooking should not be sent unless other ready-to-eat foods are also included.

193. May one send two portions of the same food?

No, the two food items must be different. However it is not necessary for the items to require two different *brachos*. For example, one may send two different cakes or two fruits etc.

194. May one send a drink?

Yes, drinks are also suitable. One may send two different drinks, or one food and one drink.

195. What is the minimum quantity of food?

The food should be of a respectable quantity according to the standards of the sender and recipient. Therefore one should send a nicer package to a wealthy person than to a poor person, and a wealthy person should send a nicer package than a poor person.

196. Is it better to send a large number of small gifts or a small number of large gifts?

One should send at least one nice package to one person and any additional packages may be small 'token' packages. This is better than sending a large number of small 'token' packages.

197. May one use *ma'aser* money to buy the food?

This is not permitted since *ma'aser* money must be used to support the poor. If a person wishes to send several packages to poor people he may use *ma'aser* money for all but the first package (see also questions 53, 172).

198. Are women obligated to send?
Yes, since they were also included in the Purim miracle.

199. May a husband and wife send jointly?
Yes. A note should be attached indicating that the package is being sent on behalf of both the husband and wife. (See also question 202.)

200. Can children who live at home be included with the parents' package?
According to some opinions, a package may be sent on behalf of the entire family. According to another opinion, only a husband and wife can send together, but children should send their own. If children prepare their own packages from food in their parents' home, they should be allowed to acquire the food before sending it.

201. Do children below bar or bas mitzvah need to send?
Children aged six or seven should be trained to perform the mitzvah (see previous question).

202. May two or more people send jointly?
Yes, but the package should contain the correct quantity for each of the senders.

203. To whom should one send packages?

It is praiseworthy to send to Jews who know little about Torah. This will arouse their interest in Jewish practices and increase love and friendship between Jews (see question 190). It is advisable to send at least one other package to an observant Jew. In a similar vein, this is an ideal opportunity to repair broken relationships by sending packages to people with whom one has ill feeling.

204. May a man send a package to a woman?

A man should send to a man and a woman to a woman, but not a man to a woman or a woman to a man. A family may send to a man or a woman, and a man or a woman may send to a family.

205. May a brother and sister living away from home send to each other?

Yes.

206. May an engaged couple send to one another?

No. The package should be addressed from or to the family.

207. May one send to a mourner?

No. If another member of the family is not in mourning, the package may be addressed to the family.

208. Is a mourner obligated to send?

Yes, but the package should not be too elaborate. According to some opinions, it is preferable to send to one person only. (See also previous question).

209. If a person receives a package, must he reciprocate and send one in return?

It is praiseworthy to do so but not an obligation.

210. May one give the package personally?

According to the prevalent custom, one may give the package personally. According to some opinions, it is preferable to send the package via a third person since the verse describes the mitzvah as **sending** food packages to one another (chapter 9, verse 22).

211. May one use a child as a messenger?

Yes, but one should confirm that the package was delivered since one may not automatically assume that the child carried out the task. If an adult delivered another package, one need not be concerned about the package sent with a child.

212. May one use a delivery service?

A reliable delivery service may be used.

213. May one send an anonymous package?

Since one of the purposes of the mitzvah is to increase love and friendship between people (see question 190), it is important for the recipient to know who sent it. Therefore, the messenger should tell the recipient who the sender is, or an identifying note should be attached to the package.

214. What if the intended recipient is not home?

- If the sender intended to give the package to a specific person, it would not be sufficient to deliver it to another member of the family (unless he is sure that the package will be given over on Purim).
- If the sender did not intend to give the package to a specific member of the family, the package may be given to anyone in the family.
- If no-one is home, it is advisable not to leave the package there, since a person would not fulfill one's obligation if the food were not received on Purim. One may risk leaving the package there if he does not rely on this to fulfill his obligation, and sends another package to someone else. (Compare question 181.)

215. May one send the package before Purim or on the evening of Purim?

- Ideally, the package should be both sent and delivered on Purim during the day.
- If the package is sent before Purim but delivered on the day of Purim, it is questionable whether he has fulfilled his obligation.
- If the package is sent and delivered before Purim or on the evening of Purim, he has not fulfilled his obligation.

216. May a person observing the 14th send a package to a person observing the 15th or vice-versa?

According to most opinions, the sender and recipient must observe the same day of Purim. If a person observing the 14th sends a package on the 14th to a friend observing the 15th and the package arrives on the 15th, he fulfills his obligation according to some opinions. Ideally, one should not rely on this. (Compare questions 108, 185.)

Chapter Twelve
Feasting and Rejoicing

217. How does one perform the mitzvah of feasting?

The main mitzvah is to have a festive meal on the day of Purim. In addition, one should have a nicer meal than usual on the evening of Purim.

218. Should one feast and rejoice equally on the 14th and 15th?

No. The main feasting and rejoicing is reserved for the main day of Purim that one observes. A person should feast and rejoice a little more than usual on the other day of Purim (see also question 265).

219. What should the evening meal consist of?

There is a custom to eat seeds and pod foods e.g. rice, peas and beans. This is in memory of Esther who ate these foods in the palace of Achashverosh in order to avoid eating non-kosher food. She was following the lead of Daniel and his colleagues who acted similarly in the palace of the king of Babylon.

Chapter Twelve – Feasting and Rejoicing

220. Should one eat meat at the evening meal?

There are different customs about this. Some refrain from eating meat to prevent people from mistakenly assuming that this is the main Purim feast.

221. Should one eat bread at this meal?

It is not necessary to eat bread.

222. What other preparations should be made for the evening?

The table should be nicely laid. Some have a custom to light candles.

223. When do those observing the 15th have the evening meal?

They should have a festive meal on the evening of the 15th, but the seed foods should be eaten on the evening of the 14th following the Fast of Esther.

224. Why do people eat Hamantaschen?

This three-cornered pastry alludes to a *midrash* which says that when Haman saw the merits of the three patriarchs, he lost his strength. The Yiddish word 'hamantasch' when written in Hebrew - המן תש - means 'Haman became weak'. The filling is usually made from poppy-seed in memory of Esther (see question 219).

225. Must one eat bread and meat at the daytime meal?

According to some opinions, one must eat bread and meat, and this is the prevalent custom.

226. Is chicken as acceptable as beef?

No, it is preferable to eat beef.

227. Should women drink wine?

Some women have a custom to drink a little wine in honor of the day.

228. Should children drink wine.

It is not necessary.

229. When should the meal be served?

The custom is to serve it in the afternoon. (See also question 233.)

230. Should one *daven mincha* before or after the meal?

One should daven *mincha* first.

231. Must the meal finish before nightfall?

No, the meal may continue into the night and some have the custom to deliberately do so. However, the main part of the meal should be eaten during the day.

232. If the meal finishes at night, should one recite *al haNissim* in *bensching*?

Yes. When Purim is on Friday and the meal continues into Shabbos, *retzei* is recited but not *al haNissim* (see question 234).

233. When should the meal be served if Purim is on Friday?

Ideally, it should be served before *halachic* midday. If this time passed, one should make every effort to begin the meal before the tenth hour (i.e. halfway between *halachic* midday and sunset).

234. May one begin the meal on Friday after the start of the tenth hour?

If a person was unavoidably delayed he may still begin the meal after the start of the tenth hour. However, because the time is close to Shabbos, he must follow one of two possible courses:

- Eat less than a regular meal and *bensch* before Shabbos, **or**
- Eat a regular festive meal and accept Shabbos during the meal. At that point he must cover the bread and make *Kiddush* omitting the *b'racha* over the wine (assuming he has already drunk wine during the meal). He must then eat at least another *kezayis* of bread in honor of Shabbos. (See also question 232).

235. How should one set the spiritual tone of the meal?

- One should spend a little time studying Torah before the meal. There is a special mitzvah to begin studying the laws of Pesach on the 14th of Adar.
- One should have in mind that eating the meal is a mitzvah.
- One should relate the Purim miracles and sing praises to Hashem.

236. How does one perform the mitzvah of rejoicing?

It is a mitzvah for men to drink wine. Unlike other *Yomim Tovim* when drinking wine is only a means to reach a state of happiness, on Purim drinking wine is itself the mitzvah.

237. Why did the Sages institute such a mitzvah?

Because the miracle of Purim occurred through feasting. Queen Vashti was removed at a feast held by King Achashverosh, and this led to the appointment of Esther as the new queen. Similarly, Haman met his downfall at a feast held by Esther, and this led to the abolishment of Haman's evil decree. Since the miracles revolved around feasts of wine, the Sages instituted the drinking of wine as a reminder of these events.

238. Is a person obligated to become drunk?

According to some opinions, there is such an obligation. In the words of the Sages, a person is required to drink until he can no longer distinguish between 'Cursed be Haman' and 'Blessed be Mordechai'. According to other opinions, one is only required to drink more than usual, but not to the point of becoming drunk. One should then go to sleep and thereby be unable to distinguish between 'Cursed be Haman' and 'Blessed be Mordechai'.

239. Which opinion should one follow?

The Sages certainly did not want people to make a fool of themselves and behave with frivolity and disgrace. The intention is to come close to Hashem, using joy to reach great heights of love and praise for Hashem. A person who knows that intoxication will prevent him from making *brachos* or *davening* properly (see question 73), or will lead him to light-headedness, should follow the second opinion and drink with moderation. Everything that one does should be purely for the sake of Heaven.

240. Can one fulfill the mitzvah with other alcoholic drinks?

It is preferable to drink wine only. A person who wishes may have other alcoholic drinks after some wine.

241. When should one fulfill this mitzvah?

The main obligation is to drink during the festive meal. If a person wishes to fulfill the mitzvah by sleeping, he should drink a little wine during the meal and go to sleep after *bensching*. Sufficient time should be left to fall asleep before nightfall.

242. What if alcoholic drinks are harmful to a person?

Then he should refrain from drinking too much. If he is able to drink a little, he should do so.

243. Why do some people wear masks and costumes on Purim?

Among the many reasons given are:
- On a superficial level, the events of the Purim story seem to be a series of natural events and fortuitous coincidences. It is only when a person digs beneath the surface and studies the story in depth that he realizes that Divine providence was constantly guiding the events. The wearing of masks and fancy costumes alludes to the fact that Hashem too was, so to speak, hiding behind the scenes. This is also one of the reasons why the name of Hashem does not appear anywhere in the megillah. In addition, the verse in the Torah which describes this phenomenon says "and I shall surely hide my face on that day" (*Devarim* 31, 18). The Hebrew words 'I will surely hide' - הסתר אסתיר closely resemble the name of Esther.
- The Talmud relates that one of the sins of the Jewish people that led to the evil decree was the bowing down to the idol of Nebuchadnetzar (see Daniel Chap. 3). However, the Jews only appeared outwardly to be worshipping the idol, but inwardly their hearts were loyal to Hashem. The wearing of disguises on Purim alludes to this scenario where the outward appearance hides the inner truth.

Chapter Twelve – Feasting and Rejoicing

244. May a male dress like a female and vice-versa?

This behavior is discouraged. There is a Torah prohibition against dressing like the opposite gender, and according to some opinions, this applies even when done in fun. One should refrain even if only one garment is switched and the remaining clothes clearly identify the person's gender.

245. May one be lenient with children below bar or bas mitzvah?

No, the law is the same for children.

246. May people steal from one another in fun?

This depends on the local custom. Even in places where the custom is to permit this, it is nevertheless recommended to refrain from such behavior.

247. Is one required to pay for accidental damages caused during the Purim festivities?

The custom is to forgo minor damages but one must pay for major damages. In case of doubt as to the seriousness of the damage, or when the damaged party is not prepared to forgive, a rav must be consulted. It is certainly forbidden to deliberately cause damage, and any such damage must be paid for.

248. What if a person insulted someone while intoxicated?

He is required to ask for forgiveness. A person is always held responsible for his actions, and drinking alcohol is not a license for disgraceful behavior (see question 239).

249. Are Purim plays and skits acceptable?

As mentioned above, it is forbidden to insult or embarrass people even in jest. To poke fun, mock or ridicule Rabbis and Torah scholars (ח"ו) is a most serious transgression, and could cause a person to lose his share in the next world. Teachers at yeshivos, seminaries, schools etc. must supervise such plays, ensuring that the scorn and derision is directed only towards the wicked (e.g. Haman, Amalek, Heretics etc.).

Chapter Thirteen
Travelling on Purim

This presentation of the laws for travelers follows the rulings of the *Mishna B'rura*. However, this topic is the subject of complex dispute. Additionally, the cases presented here are only the most basic, where a person plans a certain itinerary and actually keeps it. If a person changes his plans during the two day period of the 14th and 15th of Adar, whether by choice or by force of circumstance, he may receive a different ruling. There is an almost endless number of situations and in any case of doubt, a rav should be consulted.

250. What problems may be created by travelling on Purim?

As explained in Chapter Four, Purim is celebrated in Jerusalem on the 15th of Adar and in other cities on the 14th of Adar. However, the day that each individual is required to observe is not necessarily dependent on his usual place of residence. Based upon certain words in the megillah, the Sages instituted a new concept known as one-day-citizenship. Accordingly, whoever happens to be in Jerusalem on the 15th becomes a one-day-citizen of Jerusalem and celebrates Purim on that day, even if he usually resides in another city. Similarly, whoever happens to be in another city on the 14th becomes a one-day-citizen of that city and celebrates Purim on the 14th, even if he usually resides in Jerusalem. Therefore, it is important for a person to plan his itinerary for the two days of Purim, in order to know which day he is required to observe.

251. Based upon what time of day is a person's status determined?

His status is determined based upon his planned and actual location at *halachic* dawn. (Wherever dawn is mentioned in the following cases, it refers to *halachic* dawn.)

252. What are the rules for a person living in Jerusalem who travels to another town on Purim?

There are five basic cases:
- If he leaves Jerusalem before dawn on the 14th, intending to remain outside Jerusalem until after dawn, he observes the 14th (even if he then returns to Jerusalem after dawn). However, he may not read the megillah while still in Jerusalem on the evening of the 14th. If he returns to Jerusalem before dawn on the 15th, he will also be required to observe the 15th according to some opinions.
- If he leaves Jerusalem before dawn on the 14th, intending to return to Jerusalem before dawn, he observes the 15th.
- If he leaves Jerusalem after dawn on the 14th but before dawn on the 15th, intending to remain outside Jerusalem until after dawn of the 15th, he cannot observe Purim on either day according to many

opinions. This itinerary should be avoided. If this itinerary was unavoidable, the 14th should be kept. The person should read the megillah himself on the evening of the 14th while still in Jerusalem, in the presence of ten men.

- If he leaves Jerusalem after dawn on the 14th but before dawn on the 15th, intending to return to Jerusalem before dawn of the 15th, he observes the 15th. According to some opinions, he may not read the megillah on the evening of the 15th while outside Jerusalem.
- If he leaves Jerusalem after dawn on the 15th, he observes the 15th wherever he is.

253. What are the rules for a person living outside Jerusalem who travels to Jerusalem on Purim?

There are five basic cases:
- If he goes to Jerusalem before dawn on the 14th, intending to remain there until after dawn of the 15th, he observes the 15th.
- If he goes to Jerusalem before dawn on the 14th, intending to leave Jerusalem before dawn of the 15th, he observes the 14th (even if he is still in Jerusalem).
- If he goes to Jerusalem after dawn on the 14th but before dawn on the 15th, intending to remain in Jerusalem until after dawn of the 15th, he observes the 14th. According to some opinions, he must also observe the 15th.

- If he goes to Jerusalem after dawn on the 14th but before dawn on the 15th, intending to leave Jerusalem before dawn of the 15th, he observes the 14th.
- If he goes to Jerusalem after dawn on the 15th, he observes the 14th.

254. Why should one avoid becoming obligated to observe the 14th in Jerusalem or the 15th outside Jerusalem?

Although in certain cases this could occur (see previous questions), this situation should preferably be avoided due to the following difficulties:

- There is no megillah reading in shul and a person would be required to read the megillah himself. Only in limited cases can another person read it for such a person (see question 108).
- According to some opinions, the megillah may only be read in the presence of ten men, since in this place it is not the standard day that it is being read.
- It will be difficult to fulfill the mitzvos of giving gifts to the poor and of sending foods, since according to many opinions the sender and recipient must be observing the same day (see questions 185, 215).

Chapter Fourteen
Purim *Meshulash*

255. What is Purim *Meshulash*?

When the 15th of Adar is on Shabbos, the mitzvos of Purim are observed in Jerusalem over a period of three days; Friday the 14th, Shabbos the 15th and Sunday the 16th. This occurred in 5761 and is due to occur again in 5765 and 5768.

256. What about the rest of the world?

They observe all the laws of Purim as usual on Friday the 14th of Adar. The main difference is that the Purim feast must be held earlier than usual in order not to detract from the honor of Shabbos (see question 233).

257. What is the basic schedule for Jerusalem?

- Thursday the 13th of Adar - Fast of Esther. At night the megillah is read.
- Friday the 14th of Adar - Megillah reading, gifts to the poor.
- Shabbos the 15th of Adar - *Al haNissim* in *davening* and *bensching*. Special Purim reading in second Sefer Torah, *haftorah* of *Parshas Zachor*.
- Sunday the 16th of Adar - Sending food packages, Purim feast.

258. Why can't all the mitzvos be performed on Shabbos?

- The Sages forbade reading the megillah on Shabbos lest one accidentally carry it in a street where there is no *eiruv*. For the same reason, we do not blow the *shofar* or take the *lulav* on Shabbos.
- Gifts to the poor are always given on the same day that the megillah is read, since the poor look forward eagerly to this event.
- The Purim feast cannot be held on Shabbos since the Sages wished to institute a special day of celebration. Shabbos is not suitable since it is already sanctified by Hashem.
- Sending food packages is connected to the Purim feast (see question 190) and is therefore done on the same day.

259. When is the half-shekel given?

Although in regular years there are different customs about this (see question 49), in this special year all agree that it should be given at *mincha* on the Fast of Esther (Thursday).

260. Are there any special laws about the megillah reading?

- On Thursday evening care must be taken not to break the fast before hearing the megillah (see questions 85-89). This is unusual for Jerusalem, where people usually eat immediately after the fast and hear the megillah only a day later. Similarly, on

Chapter Fourteen – Purim Meshulash

Friday morning, care must be taken not to eat breakfast before hearing the megillah.

- Care must be taken not to say *al haNissim* on Thursday evening and Friday although the megillah is read. This is also unusual, since the two usually go together.
- According to some opinions, the *brachos* for the megillah may only be said when ten people are present (see question 101). Although the accepted custom is not so and *brachos* are said even for an individual, everyone should make an extra effort to attend a reading with ten people.
- One should wear Shabbos clothes in honor of the megillah. The custom is to wear Shabbos clothes for the entire three days, from Thursday evening until Sunday evening.
- With the *b'racha* of *shehecheyanu* that is recited on Friday morning, one should have in mind to include all the other special Purim mitzvos that will be performed on Friday and Sunday.

261. What if a person accidentally said *al haNissim* on Friday?

The mistake need not be corrected.

262. Is there any special feasting on Thursday evening?

No, but one should eat seed foods after the fast (see questions 219, 223).

263. Should one send any food packages on Friday?

According to most opinions, this mitzvah is performed on Sunday. However, according to a minority opinion, this mitzvah should be done on Friday and it is therefore praiseworthy to give at least one package on Friday.

264. What if a person forgot to give gifts to the poor on Friday?

He should do the mitzvah on Sunday.

265. Is there a mitzvah to feast and rejoice on Friday?

According to most opinions, it is no different from a regular year and there is a mitzvah to rejoice a little more than usual (see question 218). However, the main mitzvah of feasting and rejoicing is performed on Sunday.

266. Is one permitted to work on Friday?

According to some opinions the custom in Jerusalem is to refrain from work.

267. May one have a shave or haircut on Friday?

Although some opinions forbid this unless done by a gentile, the main custom is to permit it in honor of Shabbos.

268. May one cut nails on Friday?

Yes.

269. What are the special features of this Shabbos?

- *Al haNissim* is recited in *Shemoneh Esrei* and *bensching* (see questions 65, 68-70).
- Two *Sifrei Torah* are used, the special Purim section being read from the second. The *haftorah* of *Parshas Zachor* is read for the second consecutive Shabbos.
- The rav or someone competent should speak in shul about the laws of Purim and the miraculous events of the Purim story. Those who are unable to attend should study these topics themselves.

270. Should one add extra food and wine to the Shabbos meals in honor of Purim?

According to most opinions this is unnecessary, since the mitzvah of feasting is performed on Sunday. According to some opinions, one should add extra food and wine to the morning meal in honor of Purim.

271. Should one send any food packages on Shabbos?

According to most opinions, one should not do this. Just as the Sages were afraid that someone might carry the megillah in the street, so too we are afraid that someone may carry a food package in the street. Although most of Jerusalem has an *eiruv*, the concern is still valid. According to some opinions, one should nevertheless send one package discreetly to a neighbor in the same building (if there is an *eiruv*). Alternatively, one could invite a guest for Shabbos and give him the food items.

272. Is the megillah scroll *muktzeh*?

According to one opinion, a kosher megillah is *muktzeh* on this special Shabbos, since the Sages forbade its reading. The majority opinion is that it is not *muktzeh*, as on any other Shabbos.

273. Should one have a special *melaveh malkah* meal?

Yes, one should feast and rejoice a little more than usual.

274. What are the special features of Sunday the 16th of Adar?

- Food packages are sent to one another.
- The special Purim feast is held.
- Extra wine is drunk.
- Costumes are worn.
- Care should be taken not to say *al haNissim*. Some recommend saying it during *bensching* after the Purim feast at the הרחמן section.
- *Tachanun* and *lamnatzeach* are omitted.

275. Is work permitted?

Yes, all forms of work are permitted. One may also have a shave or haircut.

276. What are the laws of travelling to and from Jerusalem during this three-day period?

These laws are extremely complex and a rav should be consulted.

Glossary

Amalek - An evil nation descended from Esau.

Aneinu - prayer added to *Shemoneh Esrei* on a fast day.

Ashkenaz - West European Jewry.

B'racha (pl. *brachos*) - A blessing.

Bensch - To recite grace after meals.

Chagim - Festival days.

Chumash - Book containing the five books of Moses.

Chassid - East European Jewry.

Chutz La'aretz - The Diaspora.

Daven - To pray.

Devarim - Deuteronomy.

Eiruv - Enclosure of a public domain which transfers it into a private one in order to permit objects to be carried on *Shabbos*.

Eretz Yisrael - The land of Israel.

Erev Purim - The day before Purim.

Haftorah - Public reading from Prophets.

Halacha (pl. *halachos*) - Jewish law.

Hallel - Psalms of Praise recited on festive days.

HaRachaman - Supplication recited at the end of *bensching*.

Hashem - G-d.

Kezayis - A volume measure (approx. 30 cc).

Kiddush - Sanctification of *Shabbos* and *Yom Tov*, usually recited over a cup of wine.

Lamnatzeach - Psalm 20, recited towards the conclusion of the morning service.

Lulav - four species that are taken on *Succos*.

Ma'ariv - The evening prayer.
Ma'aser - Money separated as tithe.
Maftir - Last section of the Torah reading.
Megillah - Scroll.
Melaveh malkah - Meal eaten after Shabbos.
Midrash - Commentary on the Bible.
Minyan - Quorum of men required for communal prayer.
Mincha - The afternoon prayer.
Mishnah B'rura - The classic and accepted *halachic* work on the daily and holiday laws written by Rav Yisroel Meir HaCohen Kagan (1839-1933).
Mitzvah (pl. *Mitzvos*) - A commandment.
Moshe Rabbeinu - Moses our teacher.
Moshiach - The messiah.
Muktzeh - Item that may not be moved on Shabbos or Yom Tov.
Parsha (pl. *parshiyos*) - Section of the Torah.
Posek - *Halachic* authority.
Rav - Rabbi.
Retzei - Paragraph added to *Bensching* on Shabbos.
Rosh chodesh - The first day of the new month.
Sanhedrin - Supreme court.
Sefer Torah (pl. *Sifrei Torah*) - Hand written scroll of the five books of Moses.
Sephard - Spanish or eastern Jewry
Seudas Mitzvah - Meal eaten to celebrate a *mitzvah*, e.g. circumcision, wedding, redemption of the firstborn etc.
Shehecheyanu - The blessing made to thank *Hashem* for bringing us to the time when we can benefit

from a new item or perform a new mitzvah.

Shemoneh Esrei - Supplication that forms a central part of formal prayer. On a weekday this contains 19 blessings.

Shemos - The book of Exodus.

Shofar - Ram's horn blown at the New Year.

Siddur - Prayer book.

Succos - Feast of Tabernacles.

Tachanun - Prayer recited immediately following *Shemoneh Esrei*.

Tisha B'Av - Ninth of Av, day of mourning and fasting.

Yom Tov - Festival.

Index

A

Al haNissim
- correct version....................30
- forgot during *bensching*....................31
- forgot during *Shemoneh Esrei*....................31
- recite from a *siddur*....................31
- recited on Purim 30, 31

B

Before the megillah
- eating 36
- learning 37
- sleeping 37
- women eating....................37
- working....................37

C

Candies
- for children on fast of Esther....................18

Changes to *davening*
- fast of Esther....................21

Children
- candies on fast of Esther....................18
- dressing like opposite gender 77
- drinking wine on Purim....................72
- fast of Esther....................18
- gifts to the poor....................59
- hearing the megillah.................... 41, 50
- saying *aneinu* on fast of Esther....................21
- sending food 65

Costume
- reason behind....................76
- wearing during *davening*....................33

D

Davening
- while intoxicated 33

F

Fast of Esther
- additions to *Shemoneh Esrei* 21
- appropriate for personal requests 17
- ate by mistake 21
- *Avinu Malkeinu* 22
- bathing 22
- children fasting 18
- cleaning teeth 20
- eating before dawn 20
- fast commences 20
- feeling unwell 18
- forgot to say *aneinu* 21
- give charity if can't fast 19
- giving *machatzis haShekel* 22, 26
- ill person saying *aneinu* 21
- listening to music 22
- made *b'racha* on food by mistake 20
- reason behind 17
- rinsing mouth 19
- taking medicine 19
- tasting food 19
- women fasting 17

Festive meal
- *bensching* after nightfall 73
- both days of Purim 70
- eating before night 72
- eating bread in evening 71
- eating meat in evening 71
- obligation to become intoxicated 75
- on *erev* Shabbos 73
- Purim *meshulash* 86
- reason behind drinking 74
- what to eat during the day 72
- what to eat in evening 70
- when to drink alcohol 75
- when to eat during the day 72, 73
- when to have 70
- which type of alcohol 75

G

Gifts to the poor
- charity collector 59
- childrens obligation 59

giving to all who ask 61
giving to children 62
giving to gentiles 62
ma'aser money 58
minimum quantity 57
reason behind 57
using a check 58
when to give 60
who may receive 59
women's obligation 58

H

Haircut
    on Purim 34
    on Purim *meshulash* 86
Hallel
    reason not recited 32
Hamantaschen
    reason behind 71
Hearing every word
    megillah 47
    parshas Zachor 15

L

Laundry
    on Purim 34

M

***Ma'aser* money**
    gifts to the poor 58
    machatzis haShekel 26
    sending food 64
Machatzis haShekel
    changing custom 25
    didn't give 26
    foreign currency 24
    giving on fast of Esther 22, 26
    minimum donation 24
    reason behind 23
    three coins 23
    using *ma'aser* money 26
    which charity 25
    who is obligated 25

women's obligation 25
Matanos la'evyonim .... **See Gifts to the Poor**
Medicines
   fast of Esther 19
Megillah
   after *b'racha* 45
   attending public reading 55
   banging at Haman 55
   cannot hear on Purim 39
   children's obligation 41
   didn't hear *brachos* 45
   didn't read at all 40
   didn't read at night 38
   didn't hear a syllable 49
   didn't hear every word 48
   eating before 36
   following every word 50
   forgot to recite *brachos* 45
   hand-written 48, 49, 56
   hearing every word 47
   hearing from loudspeaker 50
   hearing with hearing aid 50
   learning before 37
   mourner reciting *brachos* 45
   muktzeh on Purim *meshulash* 88
   reading after sunrise 39
   reading along from a megillah 49
   reading before dawn 38
   reading before sunset 39
   reading from nightfall 38
   reading in correct tune 52
   roll up before after *b'racha* 54
   sleeping before 37
   speaking during recitation 51, 52
   spreading out parchment 54
   stand for *brachos* 46
   standing during 47
   ten names in one breath 53
   understand its meaning 51
   verses recited by congregation 52, 53
   verses recited twice 53
   what to think when hearing 42
   which *brachos* recited 43
   who recites *brachos* 44
   women eating before 37
   women's obligation 40

Index

working before 37
Mishloach manos.................................. See Sending food
Mourner
   receiving food 66
   sending food 67

N

Nails
   cutting on Purim 35
   cutting on Purim *meshulash* 87

P

Parshas Zachor
   calling up a child for maftir 14
   didn't hear it 15
   heard in a different pronunciation 15
   hearing every word 15
   reason it is read 13
   understand its meaning 15
   what to think when hearing 14
   women's obligation 14
Purim
   accidental damages 77
   changes to *davening* 30
   cutting nails 35
   disgraceful behaviour 78
   dressing like opposite gender 77
   haircut 34
   Hamantaschen 71
   intoxication 74
   laundry 34
   plays and skits 78
   reason behind 27
   seeds and pod foods 70
   Shabbos clothes 35
   starting to learn laws of Pesach 74
   stealing from one another 77
   two days 41, 61, 69
   working 34
   writing 35
Purim *meshulash*
   al haNissim 85
   basic schedule 83
   Festive meals 87

machatzis haShekel 84
megillah 84
megillah *brachos* 85
reason behind 84
sending food 86, 87

S

Sending food
anonymously 67
brother to sister 66
children's obligation 65
engaged couple 66
giving personally 67
ma'aser money 64
man to a man 66
minimum quantity 63, 64
mourners obligation 67
Purim *meshulash* 86, 87
reason behind 63
recipient not home 68
two different items 64
via a child 67
via a delivery service 67
when to send 68
which types of food 63
who to send to 66
women's obligation 65

Shabbos clothes
Purim *meshulash* 85
wear on Purim 33, 35

Shushan Purim
Jerusalem neighborhoods 29
reason behind 27

T

Travelling on Purim
change of itinerary 79
from Jerusalem 80
Purim *meshulash* 89
reason for problems 79
to Jerusalem 81

U

Understand meaning
   megillah 51
   parshas Zachor 15

W

Women
   drinking wine on Purim 72
   eating before megillah 37
   fast of *Esther* 17
   gifts to the poor 58
   hearing the megillah 40
   Parshas Zachor 14
   reciting *brachos* over megillah 44
   sending food 65

Work
   on the day of Purim 34
   Purim *meshulash* 86, 88

Writing
   on Purim 35

Hebrew Sources

פרק א - ד' פרשיות

[1] מ"ב ס' תרפה סק"א וס"ק טז.   [2] ס' רפ"ב סע' ד ברמ"א, ובמ"ב ס"ק כג וביה"ל שם.   [3] אשי ישראל פמ"ט סע' ח, י.   [4] מ"ב ס' תרפה ס"ק יד, הגהות חת"ס לס' תרפה, מקראי קודש ס' ב.   [5] הגר"נ קרליץ והגרח"ק ע"פ מ"ב ס' קצג סק"ה הובא בקונטרס פסקי הלכות, מועו"ז ח"ב ס' קסה.   [6] מקראי קודש ס' ז.   [7] הליכות שלמה פ"ה הע' 68, הררי קודש סו"ס ז, וע' תשובות והנהגות ח"א ס' קנד לענין קריה"ת בשבת, שהגרי"ז הקפיד בזה אבל החזו"א לא הקפיד.   [8] שיטת המג"א הובא במ' ב ס' תרפה ס"ק טז, רמ"א סוף הסימן, מועו"ז ח"ו ס' צח.   [9] מ"ב ס"ק טו.   [10] שהחיוב על הציבור ולא על היחיד. וע' אשי ישראל פל"ח הע' מה, ובהליכות שלמה פי"ב סע' א.

פרק ב - תענית אסתר

[11] מ"ב ס' תרפו סק"ב.   [12] קב הישר פ' צז.   [13] ס' תקנ סע' א.   [14] מ"ב ס' תרפו סק"ד ושעה"צ סק"י.   [15] מ"ב שם.   [16] מ"ב ס' תקנ סק"ה.   [17] בשם ר"ח מבריסק.   [18] שם סק"ה.   [19] מ"ב ס' תרפו סק"ה, מט"א ס' תרב סע' כג.   [20] שו"ת אג"מ או"ח ח"ג ס' צא, שו"ת צי"א ח"י ס' כה (פ' כב), ששכ"כ פל"ט סע' ח.   [21] ס' תקסז סע' א, מ"ב סק"ו.   [22] מ"ב ס' תקסז ס"ק יא, מט"א ס' תרב סע' ו.   [23] מנחת יצחק ח"ד ס' קט, וע"ש שמתיר להשתמש עם אבק שיניים, בלי מים.   [24] ס' תקסד סע' א, מ"ב סק"ו, שעה"צ סק"ז.   [25] מ"ב ס' פט ס"ק כז, אשי ישראל פי"ג סע' כו והערה עא בשם הגרשז"א.   [26] אלף המגן ס' תרנ ס"ק טו.   [27] ס' תקסח סע' א, מ"ב ס"ק כד.   [28] מ"ב ס' תקסח סק"ג.   [29] ביה"ל ריש ס' תקסה.   [30] שם סע' ב, מ"ב סק"ו.   [31] אשי ישראל פכ"ג הערה רב, מט"א ס' תרב סע' כה, וצ"ע מה שכתב בסידורים לומר 'רבון' בתענית יחיד דווקא דהוי נגד השו"ע ס' תקסה סע' ד, וע' מט"א שם סע' ל שאם שכח לאומרו במנחה שיכול לאומרו במעריב.   [32] איש ישראל פמ"ט סע' טו.   [33] ע' דעת תורה ס' תקפד סע' א בשם קיצור של"ה.   [34] פסקי תשובות ס' תרפו סע' ב

בשם נטעי גבריאל, שעה"צ ס' תקנ סק"ח.   [35] שם הע' 6.
[36] ס' תרצד סע' א, לוח א"י, פורים משולש להגר"ש
דבליצקי, ריש פ"ב, אדר ופורים להגר"י שוורץ, עמ' 75.

פרק ג - מחצית השקל

[37] ס' תרצד סע' א ברמ"א.   [38] שם.   [39] כן משמע
בדעת תורה ד"ה מחצית מן וכו'.   [40] שם.   [41] ביה"ל
ד"ה ויש, כה"ח ס' תרצד אות כ, שיעורין של תורה, עמ' סה,
אות יז.   [42] עיין מקורות 39.   [43] פשטות דברי הרמ"א
שם, דרך אמונה מעשר שני פ"ד הל' יד, ביה"ל ד"ה מי
בס"ד.   [44] מ"ב ס' תרצד סק"ה.   [45] מג"א סק"ג, שבה"ל
ח"ז ס' קפג.   [46] מ"ב סק"ה, מקור חיים ס' תרצד.   [47]
שע"ת סק"ב, שעה"צ סק"ט, לוח א"י.   [48] ס' תרצד סע' ד.
[49] סע' א, כה"ח ס"ק כה, לוח א"י, ע' מקורות 36.   [50]
מ"ב סק"ד, לוח א"י.   [51] ע"פ מג"א סק"ב, אדר ופורים
להגרי"ש שוורץ, עמ' 75.   [52] לוח א"י, וע' כה"ח ס"ק כא
תפלה נאה.   [53] באה"ט סק"ב בשם של"ה.

פרק ד - הב' ימים של פורים

[54] ריש מס' מגילה, מ"ב ס' תרפ"ח סק"א, תרגום אסתר
פ"ט, פט"ז, מגילת אסתר פ"ט פי"ג.   [55] שם.   [56] לוח
א"י, ס' תרפח סע' ד, כה"ח ס' תרפח ס"ק כג, בן איש חי
שנה א, הל' פורים אות יז, חיי"א כלל קנה סע' ח.   [57]
חזו"א ס' קנא וקנג, מנח"י ח"ח ס' סב, שבה"ל ח"ו ס' צג.
[58] ס' תרצה סע' ב ברמ"א, ס' תרצו סע' ג, מ"ב ס' תרצג
סק"ח.   [59] ס' תרצה סע' ב ברמ"א.

פרק ה - דיני פורים

[60] ס' תרפט, תרצד, תרצה.   [61] ס' תרצג.   [62] ס' תרפב
סע' א.   [63] מ"ב סק"א, יסוד ושורש העבודה שער יב, פ"א
בא"ד ד"ה כתוב בספרים.   [64] מ"ב ס' ק סק"א.   [65] ס'
תרפב סע' א, מ"ב סק"ד.   [66] מחבר שם.   [67] ס' תרפב סע'
א.   [68] ס' תרפב סע' א וברמ"א.   [69] מ"ב סק"ה.   [70]
מ"ב סק"ג.   [71] מסכת מגילה דף יד/א.   [72] מ"ב ס' צא,
ס"ק יב, ועיין מקורות 84.   [73] ס' צט סע' א, ומ"ב סק"ה,
י"ז.   [74] מ"ב סק"ו, י"ז.   [75] ס' תרצו סע' א.   [76] שם
ברמ"א, מ"ב סק"ג וסק"ו, שעה"צ סק"ג.   [77] מ"ב סק"ב.

[78] בן איש חי שנה א, הל' פורים אות כא. [79] מבקשי תורה ח"ג עמ' קפא בשם הגריש"א. [80] פסקי תשובה ס' ק"נ. [81] מ"ב סק"ו. [82] ביה"ל ד"ה אין עושין. [83] שעה"צ סק"ז, וע' מ"ב סק"ז. [84] ס' תרצה סע' ב ברמ"א, מ"ב סק"ג, כה"ח ס"ק יג.

פרק ו - דינים קודם קריאת המגילה

[85] ס' תרצב סע' ד ברמ"א ומ"ב ס"ק טו. [86] ס' רלה סע' ב. [87] מ"ב ס' תרצב ס"ק יד, וסו"ס רלב. [88] ס' תרצב ס"ק טז. [89] שם. [90] מ"ב ס"ק טו, שבות יצחק ח"ב עמ' שד בשם הגריש"א. [91] מ"ב ס' רלב סק"ט, ביה"ל ד"ה לבורסקי. [92] מג"א ס' תרצב סק"ז.

פרק ז - קריאת המגילה

[93] מ"ב ס' תרפז סק"ב בשם רש"י. [94] מ"ב ס' תרצב ס"ק יד. [95] מ"ב ס' תרפז סק"ג, ערוה"ש סק"ד. [96] שע"ת ד"ה חייב. [97] סע' א, מ"ב סק"ו. [98] מ"ב סק"ה. [99] ס' תרפח סע' ז, מ"ב סק"כ. [100] שם ברמ"א, מ"ב ס"ק כב. [101] שם סע' ח, מ"ב ס' תרצ ס"ק סא. [102] ר"ס תרפט ומ"ב שם. [103] מ"ב סק"ח. [104] ס' תרפט סע' ב ומ"ב סק"ז. [105] מ"ב שם, שעה"צ ס"ק טו. [106] סע' ו, ומ"ב ס"ק יז, יח. [107] סע' ב, ומ"ב סק"ו. [108] מ"ב ס' תרפח סק"ח. [109] ס' תרצ סע' יד, רמ"א ס' תרפט סע' ב. [110] מ"ב ס"ק מח. [111] מ"ב ס' ס, סק"י. [112] ס' תרצ סע' יג, מ"ב ס"ק מט.

פרק ח - ברכת המגילה

[113] ס' תרצב סע' א. [114] מ"ב סק"א, וסק"ג. [115] מ"ב סק"ג. [116] מ"ב סק"י, מנח"י ח"ג ס' נד (לז). [117] שעה"צ ס' תקפה ס"ק טו, מנח"י שם אות לח. [118] לוח א"י, מנח"י שם אות לח, וע' הליכות ביתה בפתח הבית ס' כ"ה שהגרשז"א הסכים להגרימ"ט. [119] מ"ב ס' תרפט סק"ח, שעה"צ שם ס"ק טז, מ"ב ס' תרצב ס"ק יא. [120] מ"ב ס' תרצב סק"א. [121] מ"ב סק"ו. [122] שם, ושעה"צ ס"ק יא. [123] סע' א ברמ"א. [124] מקראי קודש ס' לה, הליכות שלמה פכ"ג סק"ג. [125] פרמ"ג משב"ז סק"א, ס' תרצ סע' טז. [126] מ"ב ס' תרצ סק"א, שעה"צ סק"א.

פרק ט - שמיעת המגילה

[127] ערוה"ש סק"ג, הגרשז"א הובא בפסקי הלכות עמ' סט, וכעין דברי הרדב"ז הובא במ"ב ס' צ ס"ק כח. [128] ס' תרצ סע' א. [129] בלילה ההוא עמ' 10 בשם הגרחפ"ש, כה"ח סק"ה. [130] מ"ב סק"ה. [131] מ"ב ס"ק יט. [132] מ"ב סו"ס תרפט, ס' תרצ סע' ג, מ"ב סק"ו וס"ק יט. [133] מ"ב ס' תרצ סק"ה, סע' ה. [134] ביה"ל סע' יד ד"ה אין מדקדקין, שו"ת להורות נתן ח"ט ס' כ. [135] מ"ב ס' קמב סק"ד. [136] מ"ב סו"ס תרצב. [137] ס' תרצ סע' ד, מ"ב ס"ק יג, סוס"ק כו, וס"ק ד, בלילה ההוא עמ' 11 בשם הגריש"א. [138] סע' יב, ביה"ל ס' נט סע' ד ד"ה עם הש"ץ. [139] בלילה ההוא עמ' 11 בשם הגריש"א. [140] פשוט. [141] הליכות שלמה פכ"ב סע טו, וע"ש בהערה ביאור העניין באריכות, וכ"ד הרבה פוסקים. [142] מנחת שלמה ח"א ס' ט, מ"ב סק"ה. [143] ס' תרצ סע' ח, מ"ב ס"ק כו. [144] ביה"ל ס' צב סע' ב ד"ה קורא כדרכו, מ"ב ס"ק יב, וע' ס' תרצב סע' ב ותרצ סע' ה. [145] ס' תרצב סע' ב ומ"ב סק"ט. [146] מ"ב שם. [147] שם. [148] שעה"צ ס' קסז ס"ק מג, ימי הפורים עמ' נו. [149] שע"ת ס' תרצ. [150] מ"ב ס' תרפט ס"ק טז, ס' תרצ ס"ק נח. [151] רמ"א ס' תרצ סע' יז. [152] ס' תרצ סע' טו, צפנת פענח על הרמב"ם סוף ח"ג, הובא במקראי קודש ס' יג, [וע' מ"ב ס"ק נב שדחה המנהג,] שו"ת תשובות והנהגות ח"ב ס' שנח. [153] רמ"א ס' תרצ סע' טו. [154] מ"ב ס"ק נח, הליכות שלמה פט"ו הע' 16. [155] לוח א"י. [156] שם. [157] ס' תרצ סע' יז. [158] מ"ב ס"ק נה, ב"ח (סק"ח). [159] מ"ב ס"ק נז. [160] רמ"א סע' יז, מ"ב ס"ק נט וסק"ס. [161] סע' יח, ומ"ב ס"ק סא, סב, סד. [162] סע' יח, מ"ב ס"ק סד. [163] ס' תרצא. [164] ס' תרצ סע' ג, מ"ב סק"ז, ח. [165] רמ"א שם, שעה"צ סק"י.

פרק י - מתנות לאביונים

[166] ס' תרצד סע' א. [167] מ"ב סק"ב. [168] שע"ת סק"א, וע' מ"ב סק"ב. [169] מ"ב סק"ג בשם הרמב"ם (פ"ב, הל' יז). [170] שבות יצחק פ"ה הל' ב בשם הגריש"א. [171] שם הל' ג בשם הגריש"א. [172] מ"ב סק"ג. [173]

[174] רמ"א סו"ס תרצה, מ"ב ס"ק כה.   [174] מ"ב שם, וע"ע
ערוה"ש ס' תרצד סע' ב.   [175] שבות יצחק שם הל' א.
[176] שם.   [177] פרמ"ג א"א ס"ק יד.   [178] פשוט.   [179]
פשוט.   [180] מ"ב ס' תרצה ס"ק כב, כה"ח ס' תרצד ס"ק יח.
[181] ביה"ל ס' תרצד ד"ה לשני עניים, שו"ת משנה הלכות
ח"ד ס' פז, מ"ב ס' תרצה ס"ק כב.   [182] ערוה"ש ס' תרצד
סע' ב.   [183] בלילה ההוא עמ' 15 בשם הגריש"א.   [184]
ס' תרצד סע' ד.   [185] דינים והנהגות חזו"א פכ"א אות ח,
שו"ת דברי משה ח"א ס' לח.   [186] ס' תרצד סע' ג, יו"ד ס'
רנא סע' י, יסוד ושורש העבודה שער י"ב פרק ו', יו"ד ס' רמז
סע' ד.   [187] מ"ב סק"י.   [188] כן נראה.

פרק יא - משלוח מנות

[189] ס' תרצה סע' ד.   [190] תרוה"ד ס' קיא, מנות הלוי
(הובא במועו"ז ח"ב ס' קפו).   [191] מחבר שם.   [192] מ"ב
סק"כ, מעשה רב אות רמט.   [193] ערוה"ש סע' יד.   [194]
מ"ב סק"כ.   [195] ביה"ל ד"ה חייב לשלוח.   [196] ערוה"ש
סע' טו, תשובות והנהגות ח"ב ס' שנד.   [197] באה"ט ס'
תרצד סק"ב.   [198] רמ"א סו"ס תרצה.   [199] קונטרס מבית
לוי ט"ו עמ' לז.   [200] ע' מג"א ס' תרצה ס"ק יב, הליכות
ביתה ס' כ"ד ס"ק נה בשם הגרשז"א, ערוה"ש ס' תרצד
סק"ב.   [201] פרמ"ג א"א ס' תרצה ס"ק יד.   [202] קונטרס
פסקי הלכות ס' י, פ"א, אות י בשם הגרשז"א זצ"ל, הליכות
ביתה שם.   [203] עיין מקורות 190, תשובות והנהגות ח"ג
סו"ס רלו, משום דלא נקרא רעך לזה.   [204] רמ"א סו"ס
תרצה, בלילה ההוא עמ' 19 בשם הגריש"א.   [205] פשוט,
דלא שייך הטעם דספק קידושין, ע' מ"ב ס"ק כו.   [206]
פשוט, משום דשייך הטעם.   [207] רמ"א ס' תרצו סע' ו, פני
ברוך פכ"ט ס"ק עא בשם הגריש"א.   [208] ס' תרצו סע' ו,
מ"ב ס"ק יח, קונטרס פסקי הלכות סי' י פ"א אות ט.   [209]
פסקי תשובה ס' קמז.   [210] מ"ב ס' תרצה ס"ק יח, א"א
מבוטשאטש בסוף דבריו, תשובות והנהגות ח"ב ס' שמו
בשם ר' חיים מבריסק, דינים והנהגות לחזו"א פכ"א אות ח.
[211] חת"ס גיטין כד/ב ד"ה והא, ספר אדר ופורים עמ' 158
ע"פ שו"ת אחיעזר ח"ג ס' עג.   [212] מקור חיים סו"ס תרצד.
[213] מועו"ז ח"ב ס' קפו.   [214] ערה"ש ס' תרצה ס"ק טז,

מועו"ז ח"ב ס' קפו. [215] רמ"א סע' ד, באה"ט סק"ז, ערוה"ש ס"ק יז. [216] שמועה בשם החזו"א הובא בקונטרס פסקי הלכות עמ' קיח, שו"ת דברי משה ח"א ס' לח בשם בעל המנחת יצחק.

פרק יב - משתה ושמחה

[217] ס' תרצה סע' א. [218] עיין מקורות 59. [219] רמ"א סע' ב, מ"ב ס"ק יב, וע' אבן עזרא דניאל פ"א, פסוק ט"ו. [220] שעה"צ ס"ק יב. [221] שעה"צ סק"ד. [222] מ"ב סק"ג. [223] מ"ב ס"ק יא, ספק פורים ששולש פ"ב סע' יד, הע' לח. [224] מנהג ישראל תורה ס' תרצה אות ה. [225] ערוה"ש סק"ז, רמב"ם פ"ב הל' טו, וכן משמע בס' תרצו סע' ז, שיש חיוב לאכול בשר. [226] לקט יושר עמ' 156, וע' חיי"א כלל קד סע' ב, ונשמת אדם שם. [227] ארחות רבינו ח"ג, עמ' נח, וע"ע מועדים וזמנים ח"ב ס' קצ. [228] מועו"ז ח"ב ס' קצ. [229] מ"ב ס' תרצה סק"ח, ט. [230] רמ"א סע' ב. [231] שם. [232] סע' ג, מ"ב ס"ק טו. [233] מ"ב סק"י, וע' יד אפרים שמתיר לכתחילה עד שעה עשירית. [234] שעה"צ ס' תקבט סק"י, ס' רעא סע' ד, מ"ב ס' תרצה ס"ק טו. [235] רמ"א ס' תרצה סע' ב, מ"ב ס' תכבט סק"ב, מ"ב ס' תרצה סק"ד, יסוד ושורש העבודה שער י"ב פרק ו'. [236] ס' תרצה סע' ב, עמק ברכה עמ' קכו בשם הגרי"ז. [237] ביה"ל ד"ה חייב איניש. [238] סע' ב וברמ"א. [239] ביה"ל ד"ה עד דלא ידע. [240] מקראי קודש ס' מד ארחות רבינו ח"ג עמ' נו. [241] רמב"ם פ"ב הט"ו, מועו"ז ח"ב ס' קצ. [242] שע"ת סק"ב. [243] מנהג ישראל תורה ס' תרצו. [244] מ"ב ס' תרצו סק"ל. [245] הגרח"ק בשם החזו"א הובא בקונטרס פסקי הלכות עמ' קבט, בלילה ההוא עמ' 23 בשם הגרחפ"ש. [246] רמ"א סו"ס תרצו, מ"ב ס"ק לא. [247] רמ"א ס' תרצה סע' ב, מ"ב ס"ק יג, י"ד, וע' ערוה"ש סק"י. [248] פתחי חושן ח"ה פ"א סע' י ס"ק כח בשם היש"ש פ' המניח ס' ג. [249] שו"ת יחוה דעת ח"ה ס' נ, מועו"ז ח"ב ס' קצא, סק"ב.

פרק יג - דיני בן עיר שהלך לכרך וכו'

[250] מ"ב ס' תרפח ס"ק יב. [251] שם. [252] מ"ב שם, שבות יצחק בשם הגרי"ש"א, הליכות שלמה פט"ז הערה נה. [253] שם. [254] עיין מקורות 108, 185, 215.

פרק יד - פורים משולש

[255] ס' תרפח סע' ו. [256] ס' תרצה סע' ב ברמ"א. [257] ס' תרפח סע' ו, מ"ב ס"ק טז. [258] מ"ב ס"ק טו, יח. [259] הגרי"ח זוננפלד בסדר פורים משולש אות א. [260] רמ"א סו"ס תרצב, מ"ב ס' תרפח ס"ק יז וס' תרצ ס"ק סא, חזו"א ס' קנה סק"ב, הגרי"ח זוננפלד בסדר פורים משולש אות ב, ג, ד, ו. [261] מ"ב ס"ק יז. [262] מ"ב ס' תרצה ס"ק יא. [263] מ"ב ס"ק יח, חזו"א ס' קנה סק"א ד"ה ולהאמור. [264] פורים משולש להגר"ש דבליצקי פ"ח סע' י. [265] הגרי"ח זוננפלד בסדר פורים משולש אות ד. [266] ס' תרצו סע' ב, כה"ח ס' תרפח ס"ק מט. [267] שו"ת יבי"א ח"ו ס' מז, וע' כה"ח ס' תרצו ס"ק יא. [268] פסקי תשובה ס' קנ. [269] ס' תרפח סע' ו, מ"ב ס"ק טז. [270] מ"ב ס"ק יח, שעה"צ סק"ל, הגרי"ח זוננפלד בסדר פורים משולש אות ה. [271] הגרי"ח זוננפלד שם. [272] מ"ב שם, חיי"א כלל קנה סע' י, שע"ת ס' תרצג סק"א. [273] מ"ב ס' תרצה סק"ג, וע' משך חכמה סוף מגילת אסתר שדייק מהירושלמי שזה זמן סעודת פורים, וע' מקראי קודש ס' נג. [274] מ"ב ס' תרפח ס"ק יח, מקראי קודש סו"ס נב בהג"ה. [275] פורים משולש להגר"ש דבליצקי פ"ח סע' יג. [276] ע' פסקי תשובות ס' תרפח אות יב.

לע"נ

ר' חיים ליב
ב"ר משה לואיס ז"ל

נפטר בשיבה טובה
ח' תשרי תשס"ב

נתרם על ידי אשתו

ଓଃ ୨୦

Dedicated for the Iluy Nishmas of
our loving Parents and Grandparents

יעקב בן משה ז"ל
עטא בת איליעס ע"ה

May their memory be blessed

Gedaliah and Chana Chassia
Shofnos and Family

In cherished memory of
our beloved parents
Jack and Ethel Dian

ר' יעקב מאיר ב"ר ישעיהו ז"ל
נפטר ט' אייר תשס"א

מרת עטל בת ר' שלום משה ע"ה
נפטרה י"ט שבט תשנ"ד

Deeply mourned and sadly missed.
Always in our hearts.

*Shelley Weiss
Jeffrey and Larry Dian*

ରେ ଚ

לע"נ

מרת חיה דבורה בת אברהם

לע"נ

מרת אדל
ובנותיה לאה ומחל

Dedicated to my loving wife
of 57 years

Lillian Milkin
רחל זלטי בת ר' יהושע חיים עמו"ש

with great appreciation

Irvin Milkin
ר' יצחק חיים בן ר' אברהם מאיר

ஐ ஜ

May the joy of Torah
fill the hearts of
our children and
grandchildren

Akiva and Hinde Gordon

לע"נ

מרת צי‎פא בילא בת
ר' מרדכי דוד ע"ה

ר' יצחק צבי בן
ר' מרדכי דוד ז"ל

ଛ ଓ

לע"נ

ר' שלמה ב"ר משה ז"ל

מרת רייזל דבורה בת
ר' יעקב מרדכי ע"ה

ר' יצחק ב"ר זאב ז"ל

In memory of

ר׳ יעקב ב״ר אברהם ז״ל

ଓ ଃ

Dedicated to our
Beloved Leader
Rabbi Zvi Hirsch Lieberman
שליט״א

By his congregation
ק״ק עדת ישראל, עדז׳שווער

ଓ ଃ

Dedicated to the Committed
Members of the
Neveh Yaakov Community Kollel
who come and learn
with mesirus nefesh
after a hard day's work

לע"נ

מרדכי בן יאיר

אסתר בת אביחיל